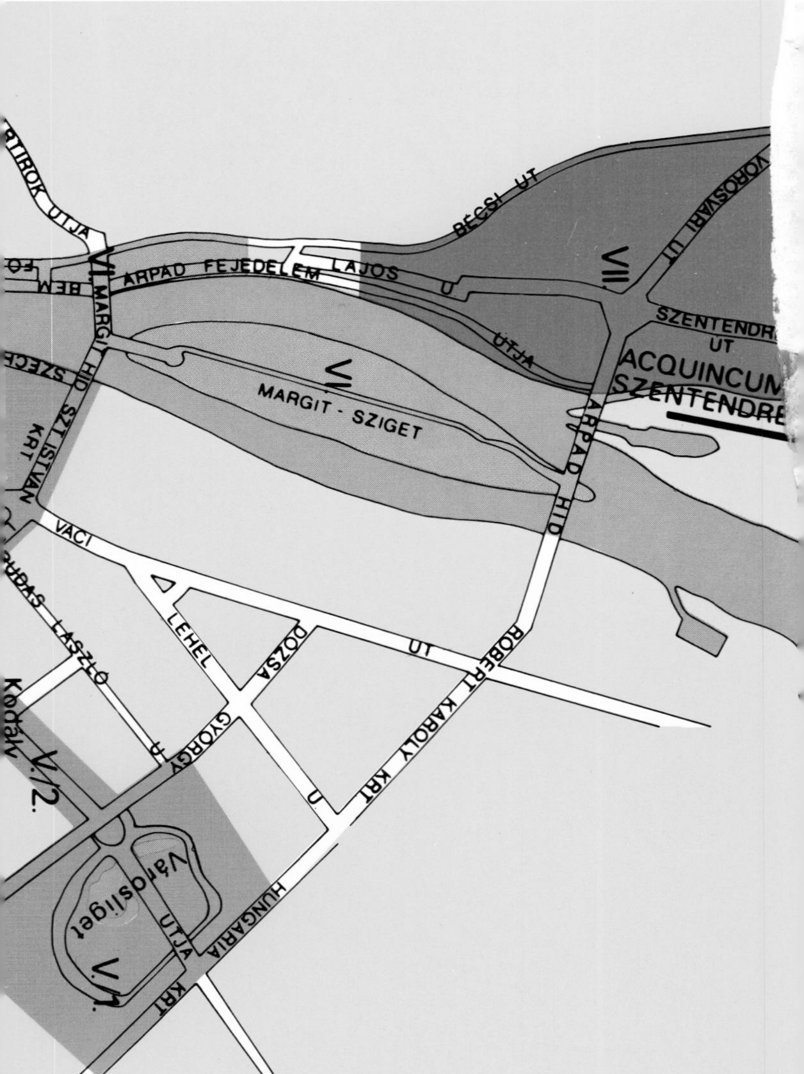

RTIROK ÚTJA
BEM
VI. MARGIT HÍD
ÁRPÁD FEJEDELEM
LAJOS
U.
ÚTJA
BÉCSI ÚT
VII.
VÖRÖSVÁRI ÚT
SZENTENDREI ÚT
ACQUINCUM
SZENTENDRE
SZT. ISTVÁN KRT.
VI.
MARGIT - SZIGET
ÁRPÁD HÍD
VÁCI ÚT
LEHEL U.
DÓZSA GYÖRGY U.
RÓBERT KÁROLY KRT
LÁSZLÓ
Kodály
V./2.
Városliget
V./1.
ÚTJA
HUNGÁRIA KRT

My Hungary

Your Guide to Budapest

Téka

Text by: **Katalin Pallai**
Edited by: **Tamás Déri**
Revised by: **Margit B. Szűcs, Margit Pásztói, Attila Pók**
Translated by: **Susan K. Kutor**
Translation revised by: **Margit B. Szűcs**
Illustrations by: **Annamária Fábián, Katalin Pallai,**
   István Péterfy
Maps by: **Edit Rózsa**
Technical editor: **Tibor Vara**

ISBN 963 7357 16 5
ISSN 0238−5090

Contents

Key to Signs

3   The number in the text, on the pictures and on the maps of the sights and the monuments mentioned

》 **《**   The description of the sight or monument

3—5   The numbers of the sights and monuments described on the page

I. Dedication

Let me tell you about my book. It is a guide book, but a guide book of very different sort. It is not just about a city I have studied, but about a city I love. Consequently it is written not in the usual detached style but very much from my heart.

Also the tone of my book often changes back and forth between serious and light. This is because while I certainly wanted to share the many delightful stories about the daily lifes of past and present residents of Budapest, I also wanted to make some serious points about how a city can develop, be destroyed and be rebuilt again, thus showing something of the very workings of history itself.

I hope you will enjoy my serious yet playful book and I hope even more that after we have finished our walk together you will forever have something of my city in your heart.

I am he who for a hundred thousand year
Has gazed on what he now sees the first time.
One brief moment and, fulfilled, all time appears.
In a hundred thousand forbears' eyes and mine.

I see what they could not for their daily toil,
Killing, kissing as duty dictated,
And they, who have descended into matter,
See what I do not, if truth be stated.

We know of each other like sorrow and joy,
Theirs is the present and mine is the past;
We write a poem, they're holding my pencil
And I feel them and recall them at last.

Attila József: By the Danube
translated by András Székely

Anno 1602

View of Pest and Buda
(engraving of Siebmacher)

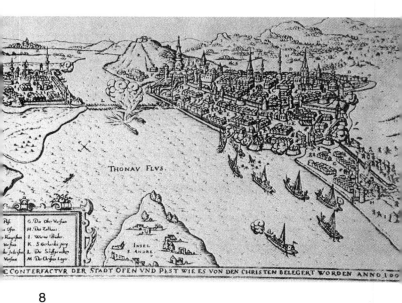

II. The History of Budapest

What better place is there to start to get to know Budapest than the **bank of the Danube**? Right **downtown** (see map **4** between **23** and **32**) we can sit on the embankment and view the entire central area of the city as well as the Danube, which has flowed tranquilly past this place for centuries, and which has often played the leading role in history. It is not merely by chance then that we have chosen this spot to sit down and think back over the events which have taken place in this region throughout the ages.

Our story begins on the opposite side—the right, or west, bank—with the arrival some 500,000 years ago of prehistoric man, who took refuge in the caves in the hills, made stone tools for themselves and lived simple lives as hunters and gatherers. After these early inhabitants, the area remained deserted for a long time until various tribes gradually began to settle in the region from around 1000 B.C. These peoples lived in primitive settlements and fought among each other until they were conquered by the Romans in the first century A.D. By then a large part of the known world belonged to the powerful Roman empire, and trade links tied even more distant lands to it. The Roman province of Pannonia was established in the western part of present-day Hungary with the Danube as its natural boundary. The Romans built roads and cities and were the first to organize the area into administrative regions, laying the foundations of many cities found even today in western Hungary. The Romans also set up a military defense system in Pannonia. The Danube formed an important natural boundary in this system as it was easily defendable with only minor reinforcements. Military encampments were established near the river with watch towers on the look-out for any invaders. The area around Budapest was built up in this way too.

The military camp of **Aquincum** (see map **7** between **79** and **82**) for instance, was located somewhat to the north of present-day Budapest where the hills sloped gently down to the Danube. Built on a walled-in flat area measuring 480 × 520 meters (1600 × 1700 feet), the camp at its height housed 6,000 soldiers. In time, military and civilian settlements with a total population of 30,000 formed around it to tend to its needs. Aquincum became the headquarters for the Roman procurator and one of the largest and most flourishing cities of all of Pannonia. It boasted all the characteristics of the life and culture of the Roman empire in all its glory: public buildings and baths, villas and palaces. Later, a bridge was also erected and two fortresses were built on the opposite bank to be used in case of attack, but the camp itself was never moved.

We know from history that by the end of the fourth century the Roman empire had expanded to the point where it became impossible to govern and control effectively despite the excellent administrative system and extensive network of roads. Inevitably, it became vulnerable to attack and began to decline. It was also natural that the outlying provinces were conquered first: the territories of present-day Germany, Austria and Hungary. The barbarian invaders eventually reached as far as Rome, and by the fifth century had completely crushed the Empire.

It was late in the fourth century when the first wave of barbaric tribes migrating from the east reached Pannonia and attacked the flourishing Roman settlements. After ravaging the towns, the tribes lived on among the ruins for a time. Throughout the centuries to come various tribes and peoples came and went until the ninth century when the fierce Magyars conquered the region. From this time on it was the Hungarians' turn to keep, or to strive to keep, control of the area.

10

As the Danube was not the boundary of their country as it was for Pannonia, but was situated in the middle, they did not want to defend the territory but to make their homes here. The Magyars were a community of nomadic tribes but kept animals and farmed the land as well. For this reason they chose to settle primarily along the rivers and on flat land and built their villages throughout the area.

Pest at that time was a swampy, sparsely populated area where the Danube, having left the hills behind, grew somewhat tamer and split off in several branches. This afforded the perfect site for a river crossing, which was located somewhere near today's Elizabeth Bridge (Erzsébet híd) (see map **4 69**). For centuries traders or tired wanderers would break their journeys here and could be assured of safe transport from one half of the country to the other for themselves and their wares or belongings. As the land Pest was built on was unsuitable for agriculture, the people turned to the opposite side of the river for food and tillable land. This was the birth of the twin cities on the two banks of the Danube.

In the centuries following the founding of the state in the year 1000, Hungary went about the business of building a nation. In this settlement too, as elsewhere throughout the country, a small church and churchyard were built, and the people prospered over the years from the trading and the ferry traffic. More than two hundred years passed in relative peace until 1241, when Mongol invaders staged a surprise attack on the defenseless country, and conquered and burned a great portion of it, slaughtering the population in the process. The king fled after the sounding defeat of the Hungarian military forces, and as no remedy was found to cure Hungary of the Mongols, prayed to God for help. Both Pest and the west bank of the Danube fell to the Mongols, but were saved from further destruction by an unexpected event. The chief Khan of the Mongols passed away suddenly and Batu Khan, the commander of the western army, immediately returned home with his soldiers to take part in the "elections."

King Béla IV returned to the ruins of a country which had lost nearly half its population and began the enormous task of rebuilding the nation. The horrendous lesson he had been taught was that islands and earthworks did not provide adequate protection. He ordered the towns to be reinforced with stone walls and he resettled his own capital city in a place which afforded better protection, the hill of Buda.

This one and a half kilometer (one mile) long natural limestone plateau rose 50–60 meters (160–200 feet) above the level of the Danube in the last one million years during the Pleistocene Age. Before the Mongol invasion the hill was merely the site of a small village. Now all of a sudden it had become the center of the nation. And in the next 750 years it grew into the city known throughout the world for its beauty which you can see on the opposite side of the river.

From your seat on the bank of the Danube you can see the northern end of the hill where King Béla IV built a royal residence, somewhat to the right of the church tower (see map **2**   **4**). Following the dictates of the new era, the citizens of Pest gradually began to move to the more easily defendable hill.

Later, in the 14th century, a Royal Palace (see map **3** between **12** and **20**) was built in its present location at the southern end of the hill, and its ramparts were fortified against increasingly more powerful weapons. At the other end of Castle Hill, the people of the civilian town of Buda worked hard at their trades and at improving their homes and town. Consequently, by the 16th century Buda was not only the capital of Hungary and the site of the royal court, but also ranked as one of the most densely populated settlements. 400 stone houses dotted the plateau, which was surrounded by multiple stone ramparts fortified with round bastions.

However impregnable the Buda castle seemed, it proved impossible to defend against the Turks. In 1541 the Turks took both towns and in the ensuing 150 years of their occupation not much was built with the exception of a few thermal baths, which are still in use today. Almost everything else was destroyed as a result of the battles and occupation. Thus, the liberation of Buda in 1686 left the Hapsburgs, who had incorporated Hungary in their empire, to reign not over twin cities but over "twin ruins."

Life slowly began to return to the country, the center of which was now Vienna. In Pest—Buda, as the twin cities were then called, the people lived simple lives on a provincial level. Real change came only later in the 19th century when a Hungarian national consciousness began to emerge. For this feeling to develop, however, a common point was needed, a city in the heart of the country which would attract, organize and act as the true center for newly awakening Hungarians. It was these enlightened Magyars who turned the small town of Pest—Buda into a flourishing city in a mere 100 years.

By the late 19th and early 20th centuries the castle walls no longer provided real protection for Buda, and instead restricted the growth of the city. The growing metropolis crossed the river again, returning to the flat land on the opposite bank which offered unlimited room for expansion. The heart of the city was once more situated on the left bank of the Danube, and Pest grew at an incredible rate. In this time of political stability, more money and energy were left over to spend on the city. Finally, in 1873 the twin cities united with a third, Óbuda, to finally be christened Budapest. Public buildings, avenues, boulevards, a sewer system and public lighting, horse-drawn trams, an underground railway, parks and bridges—all these turned the town into the impressive city which by the turn of the century was deservedly known as the "Paris of the East" or the "Queen of the Danube." Dynamic Pest evolved into the administrative, political, business and cultural center, whereas the Castle District in Buda retained its enchanting historical atmosphere.

All this was changed abruptly by the Second World War. During the war, and especially the long siege of 1944−45, 74% of the buildings in Budapest were damaged, but reconstruction work began as soon as peace returned. The guiding principle in this important task was to restore the buildings to their original state whenever possible and to preserve the historical atmosphere of the city.

Budapest reached its present size of 525 square kilometers (200 square miles) in 1950 when several suburbs were incorporated. One-third of this area lies in Buda, two-thirds in Pest, and the city is divided into 22 administrative districts. Out of the ten and a half million Hungarians living in Hungary today, 2.3 million live in the capital city of Budapest.

Budapest today still reflects its roots in the past. The centuries-old heart of Buda is a focal point for culture and tourism, while the inner city in Pest has become the center of business. To the north of the downtown area are the government offices and main state institutions, and on both sides of the river the inner sections of the city are surrounded by residential areas. While Pest is a densely packed urban center, the hills on the Buda side remain a less crowded area of homes, villas, parks and gardens. Housing complexes form a ring on the outskirts of the city, and at the southern and northern end two industrial areas have been built up alongside the Danube.

All told, Budapest is an extremely bustling and crowded city. All the main highways and the railways converge here, and this is where the only international airport and pier are located. Budapest is truly the largest city in Hungary, its heart and center.

Anno 1790

View of Buda
(engraving of G. Hisler)

III. The Castle District in Buda

1. The History of the Castle District

All the streets leading to the Castle District in Buda wind their way up to the plateau on top of a hill rising 50–60 meters (160–200 feet) high. As you climb up the steep streets, you can see the remains of the ramparts which once surrounded the entire hill, and appreciate the effectiveness of both the natural and man-made features which protected the castle and town of Buda.

After experiencing the devastation caused by the Mongol invasion, the survivors searched for a place where they could live in times of peace, but which could be defended well in times of war. Although Castle Hill was merely a narrow plateau, the system of underground caves hidden throughout it would provide shelter if needed, and fresh water welled up through the layers of limestone. Even the "quarry" was brought to their doorstep as the stone excavated during the digging of the cellars could be used to build the houses. This was the perfect site for a city intent on surviving in the Middle Ages. It is no wonder then that King Béla IV, rightfully called "the second founder of Hungary," chose this hill as the new site of his royal residence in the middle of the 13th century.

The building of the town proceeded at a feverish pace: roads were planned, plots of land were staked out, city walls, churches, houses, and even a royal residence were built. The citizens of the once flourishing city of Pest gradually began to move inside its protective walls. In moving they forfeited the trade and taxation rights of a free city that the King had bestowed upon them, but in return they no longer had to fear a renewed attack by the Mongols.

Two churches were also soon erected in the town. The Church of St. Mary Magdalene (Mária Magdolna-templom) (see map **2 8**) was built at the northern end where the Hungarians lived near the king's residence. Today only the tower of this church remains standing. The Church of Our Lady, commonly known as the Matthias Church (Mátyás-templom) (see map **2 4**), which served for many years as the royal chapel, was used by the Germans who lived in the middle of Castle Hill. The Jewish neighbourhood, on the other hand, was located further to the south near today's Parade Square (Dísz tér) (see map **2 2**), and the southern end of the plateau was again inhabited by Hungarians. These peoples went about their lives in safety inside the walls of the town, pursuing their trades, holding markets and fairs, and farming the surrounding hillsides. Apart from providing for their safety, the king did not grant them any priveleges but placed them under the authority of the church. This resulted in a continuous struggle by the citizens of Buda for their rights which peaked in an enormous scandal around the turn of the 14th century.

Around this time, the first dynasty of kings in Hungary died out, and some Hungarian barons gave the crown to Charles Robert of Anjou from the powerful French–Italian family of Naples. Other barons, together with the inhabitants of Buda, supported another pretender to the crown, and defended Castle Hill for years against the king, ample proof of how well-fortified it was. In the meantime, the events culminated in the scandalous event known as the "Buda Schism." The enraged citizens of Buda, who had been repeatedly excommunicated by the Pope and their chaplain in Óbuda, made the courageous decision in 1303 to excommunicate not only the chaplain and the king, but the Pope as well.

Five years later Charles Robert finally managed to capture Castle Hill and put an end to the struggle. He then exacted cruel revenge on his adversaries and, leaving no doubt in anyone's mind, had himself crowned again in their church. Several years later a powerful baron attacked the king and, contrary to all expectations, the people of Buda rallied to protect their sovereign leader from what would have been certain defeat. In return, the king took the final step toward reconciliation when he moved his residence from the town to the southern end of Castle Hill. In exchange for the land on which the palace was built, Charles Robert granted the citizens the rights of a free town for which they had yearned for a hundred years. All this was registered in the Buda Book of Laws at the end of the 14th century.

From this time on relative peace reigned over Castle Hill, which was now divided into two parts, the Royal Palace and royal grounds in the south, and the free civilian town in the north. The people went about their everyday lives and in so doing left their mark for centuries to come. Many of the buildings which they so carefully built and remodelled were lived in for centuries, and parts of some can still be seen today; the wells which were dug at that time were still in use a hundred years ago; and the street system planned then is still used today.

In the 15th century, King Sigismund of Luxemburg (Zsigmond, King of Hungary 1387–1437 and Holy Roman Emperor 1433–1437) began extensive reconstruction of the old walls of Buda, which had become outdated as a result of the widespread introduction of gunpowder. Not only did he embellish the Royal Palace in a manner befitting his rank, he also reinforced the walls of the town. Double stone walls packed with earth, reaching in places a thickness of 4 to 5 meters (13–16 feet), made the city invincible once again. As the Turkish menace threw its shadow over all of Europe, even the Danube was reinforced with enormous chains stretched between round bastions to protect the city from an enemy approach from the river.

For 150 years Buda reigned as the "golden city" of

Hungary. In the 15th and 16th centuries this vibrant city boasted 400 houses, weekly markets, fairs attended from all over the country, monasteries, seven schools, and even a short-lived university.

It was in this period that Hungary's most outstanding king reigned, Matthias Corvinus (Hunyadi Mátyás, 1458–1490). King Matthias was not only a resolute ruler and excellent diplomat but, in keeping with the spirit of the Renaissance, he was extremely well educated and a generous patron of the arts and sciences. During his reign the Royal Palace in Buda soon became one of the most magnificent Renaissance palaces in all of Europe and rivalled the most splendid courts in Italy. Numerous prominent people stayed for varying lengths of time at the court of King Matthias and helped to create a center of learning which became the focal point and nucleus of the spreading of Renaissance culture in Central and Eastern Europe.

This golden age was cut short by the death of King Matthias, and the country gradually started to decline. During the 150 years of Turkish occupation that followed most of the evidence of the splendor of the reign of King Matthias was destroyed forever. The magnificent Royal Palace was gradually destroyed when the powder magazine exploded several times, the final blow coming with the siege of 1686. The Franciscan monastery was converted into the palace of the pasha, and the churches were turned into mosques. The greater portion of the population of the town was also decimated by the Turks as a great percentage of the people were killed or fled.

After the reconquest of Buda in 1686 the Austrians who entered the city saw only buildings lying in ruins and mere remnants of a population. The repair of the fortifications was begun at once as the Turks still occupied southern Hungary and another attack was feared.

By the 18th century the Turks had finally been completely repulsed, and the reconstruction of the city could be begun. A new royal palace, numerous houses, churches and monasteries were built in a Baroque style imported from Vienna with the help of several famous and many less famous architects and artists. This period created the Castle District as we know it today, since the construction wave of the 19th century affected mainly Pest on the east bank, and only a few buildings were added on the hill.

Throughout its 800 year history, the Castle District has suffered 23 armed sieges and 3 devastating fires. Still, perhaps only the Turkish occupation did more damage than the Second World War. During the siege of 1944−45 the Germans retreated to the Castle District as a last resort, and in their attempt to hold it showed little concern for the historical value of the area. When the Germans were finally forced to surrender, a sorrowful scene awaited the liberating troops. Out of the 4 floors of the Royal Palace, at most 2 were still standing; out of the 200 buildings in the city, 42 were completely destroyed and more than half had been severely damaged; and in the entire Castle District only one lone small building had escaped with only having its windows broken.

Still, as is almost always the case, in the midst of this great catastrophe something interesting came to light. Collapsed cellars and damaged walls revealed forgotten remains from the 13th, 14th and 15th centuries. Complete halls, vaults, Gothic seats in niches (sedilia), portals and wells were rescued from the debris where they had been buried, walled over or altered and completely forgotten over the years as the buildings were remodeled. These elements, which—in keeping with the guidelines of modern preservation of historic monuments—are presented side by side, reveal to us many interesting and new details of life and culture of Buda in the Middle Ages.

2. Sights to see in the Castle District

» Let's begin our walk in the Castle District at **Szent György tér** (St. George's Square), which can be reached by taking the Sikló, the funicular railway, or by walking from the parking lot. This square stands on the border between the two parts of the hill: the Royal Palace to the south and the civilian city to the north. Here you can see the remains of the medieval wall which separated them. A dry moat ran in front of the wall, behind it stood a huge marketplace, followed by another wall. Before the Turkish invasion, behind this wall stood the Gothic and Renaissance palace, which was further protected on the hillside by ramparts and walls. Thus, uninvited guests were effectively kept out unless they came by the thousands as did the Turks. On the other side of the wall the town extended to the northern edge of the plateau, and was also surrounded by walls. **«**

» The large yellow building on the Danube side of the square—now the **Castle Theater** (Várszínház)—has had a most varied history indeed. In the 13th century the Franciscans, a newly-arrived mendicant order of friars, built one of the most eminent churches and

monasteries in medieval Buda. When Buda fell to the Turks, the monastery was converted into the palace of the pasha, and its church was turned into a mosque. After the reconquest of the city, both buildings were turned over to the Carmelite nuns, and when their order was dissolved in 1784 by József II, laymen took final possession of the building. The royal decree also stipulated that a casino be established in the former convent and a theater in the former church for the officers of the garrison and the employees of the government institutions which had moved to Buda. Farkas Kempelen, the famous Hungarian inventor of an automatic chess machine, drew up the ingenious plans for the theater.

To this day actors perform on the stage set up in the former apse and the audience, sitting under the arches of ages long past, revels in the wonderful acoustics. One of the most famous events connected with this building is commemorated by a relief of Beethoven to the right of the entrance. On May 7, 1800 Beethoven himself played the piano in his famous Sonata for Piano and French Horn in F major.

The facade of the theater was restored in the Baroque style of the late 18th century; the monastery, in the neo-Classical style of the middle of the 19th century. ◀◀

▶▶ If you walk parallel to the Danube in the direction of the city, you will arrive at the site of the **old town gates.** What little remained of them from the Middle Ages was completely torn down in the 19th century, and today only modern fragments mark the place where they once stood. Two gates, one opposite the other, were situated where the hill narrows slightly. The one to the east was called the **Water Gate** (Vízi kapu), the one to the west was called the **Fehérvár Gate** (Fehérvári kapu). Leaving nothing to chance, these gates provided multiple means of protection. On the outside there were dry moats; spanning them were drawbridges which blocked the gates when pulled up; behind them were iron bars which could be let down; and last of all were huge double wooden doors with iron braces which could be closed shut against the enemy. Woe be to those who arrived after the closing of the gates in the evening. Strict order was kept on Castle Hill—whoever came late, stayed outside! Altogether there were three large gates to the Castle District where wagons could enter and several smaller gates for people entering on foot. **«**

A large square stood behind the two gates in the Middle Ages and can be seen there even today. True to its name, **Dísz tér** (Parade Square) has been the site of countless fairs, processions and military parades over the centuries. In the middle of Dísz tér stands the **Soldier's Memorial** (Honvédszobor; György Zala, 1893), which commemorates the heroes of the 1848–49 War of Independence and the Siege of Buda in 1849. Let's walk over to it to have a good view of the whole square.

You are now standing in the Castle District at the edge of the city of Buda. Two streets lead up the slope and later

2

branch off into four, coming together again at the other end of the hill. It was in these same streets that the hustle and bustle of life in the Middle Ages took place. The shops opened onto the streets, each neighborhood offering its own speciality. Three times a week the activity increased even further on market days. Stalls were lined up from here all the way to the Matthias Church (Mátyás-templom) where vendors could sell their wares. On Wednesdays the Germans held market, on Fridays the Hungarians, and on a third day the Jews sold unclaimed goods from pawnshops. Twice a year fairs were held when people flocked from all parts of the country to buy and sell and make merry. In those days a large fair was a great cause for celebration. People arrived early on carts, on horseback, by boat and on foot. The animals were left outside the walls, and inside the people grouped together according to what they were selling. The bargaining and bartering went on for two continuous days. But the frenzied chaos typical of markets in the East was missing, as the rules were set down in law; and although the tax collectors might be given a good licking at night, during the day order generally prevailed.

An interesting law can be read in connection with this in the 15th century Buda Book of Laws. If one stall-keeper started to quarrel with another, a big stone was tied to her back, which she had to carry from one square to the other while the injured party poked her in the behind with a pointed stick. But the dispensing of justice was a serious matter indeed, and to prove that the law also proclaimed that if the other stall-keeper made fun of the one being punished, they traded places. The people at the fairs were treated not only to punishment of this kind, but to jugglers, acrobats, sword and flame swallowers as well. And in the evening, following a hard day's work, the fun began in earnest with lively music, crowded pubs and spirited dancing.

After our glimpse of life in the Middle Ages, let's return to the city of today. If you stand beside the **Soldier's Memorial** (Honvédszobor), you can view at a glance the relationship between past and present. On the left you can see mainly Baroque palaces reflecting the architectural fashion of the 18th century. On the right you can see an interesting building at **12 Dísz tér.** In the wall beside the gate a second gate appears to begin, and begin it did in the 14th century. The Gothic building was destroyed during the Turkish occupation and was later rebuilt. The original doorway, however, was walled over and forgotten until this old section came to light in the destruction caused by World War II. It has now been incorporated in the wall as a part of the history of the building.

A little further to the left the facade of the building at **7 Tárnok utca** seems to include beautiful ornamental pillars. But if you look closer you can see that they are only painted on the wall. This building reflects a sorrowful period in the recent past when 74% of the buildings in the Castle District were destroyed in the Second World War. In many cases the buildings could only be reconstructed from old drawings. And if totally demolished, they were replaced by completely modern ones such as the one behind the statue at **8 Dísz tér.**

Following our meanderings in the story of the restoration of the buildings, let's start up **Tárnok utca,** going towards the center of the Castle District, **Szentháromság tér** (Square of the Holy Trinity). You must head "in the direction of the tower," as Hungarians would have said in the days when towers were used as points of reference instead of traffic signs. The tower in this case is that of the Matthias Church, and the street we are walking on was one of the busiest streets in the Middle Ages.

On the left you can see the geometric design from the 16th century painted on the upper part of the facade of the building at **No. 14.** This is one of the oldest buildings still standing in the Castle District. Its cellar and ground floor date back to the 14th century; the second story, which rests on projecting consoles, was added later in the 15th century.

The next building at **No. 16** was the home of the **Golden Eagle Pharmacy** (Arany Sas Patika) from 1740 when it succeeded the first pharmacy in Buda, which was established in 1687. Today a quaint little museum can be found here which exhibits objects from the 16th to the 19th century related to pharmaceutical science. (Open: Tues–Sun from 10.30 to 5.30.)

» At the next corner you will arrive at the "tower" you were headed for at **Szentháromság tér** (Square of the Holy Trinity). The square received its name from the **Holy Trinity Column** (Szentháromság-oszlop; Fülöp Ungleich, 1712–14) in the middle erected in memory of the

3

epidemics of the plague in the 17th and 18th centuries. It was the custom in Central Europe at that time for the survivors of the plague to show their gratitude to God by erecting a magnificent monument in the main square of the city. The people of Buda too erected this enormous statue in 1712–1714 in place of an older and smaller one, probably in the hope of being granted better protection against the recurring epidemics. **《**

》 Throughout history, Szentháromság tér has been the most important place in the life of Buda. Ever since the 13th century the Matthias Church has graced this site, and since the 14th century the **Town Hall** (Városháza) has stood opposite it.

Construction on the present building was begun in 1692 on the foundations of the old Gothic town hall and other Gothic buildings. It was designed in a dignified early Baroque style by the Italian architect Andrea Ceresola. Below the clock tower which you can still see today there used to be a separate small chapel, and below that a prison and an extensive system of cellars. A statue of the patron of cities, Pallas Athene can be seen on the corner of the building holding the coat of arms of Buda. **《**

》 On the other side of the square stands one of the most important buildings in the Castle District and all of Buda, the Church of

Our Lady as it is officially named, but which is better known as **Matthias Church** (Mátyás-templom). This was the first church on Castle Hill, and was begun by King Béla IV from 1255–1269. It first served as the royal chapel and later as the parish church of the Germans who lived in the Castle District.

In 1308 the church was the site of an important event in Hungarian history. It was here that Charles Robert of Anjou, who was mentioned earlier (see page 31) was crowned King of Hungary for the second time. It was a custom in the Middle Ages in Hungary that the king was only legitimate if crowned with the crown of St. Stephen by the Archbishop of Esztergom in the Basilica in Székesfehérvár. However, in the confusion of 1301 the crown fell into the hands of the other pretender to the throne, so the Archbishop crowned Charles Robert with one borrowed from a religious statue. This was reason enough for the contenders not to recognize him as king and to spark off a struggle for the throne which would last seven years. One of the events in this contention was the Buda Schism already mentioned; the final act was the third coronation ceremony held in 1310, this time according to tradition with the recovered crown of St. Stephen. From that time on it became a tradition for the leaders of Buda to accompany the newly crowned king from Székesfehérvár to Buda to formally present the king first to the people of Buda in the Matthias Church. Consequently, the church acquired great importance and was further embellished and enlarged. At the turn of the 14th and 15th centuries it was remodelled into a hall church with a nave and side aisles, and in the 1470s King Matthias further enlarged it with the addition of a royal oratory and the magnificent southwestern tower still partially intact today.

Work on the Matthias Church was more or less completed by the 15th century, and only minor adaptations have been made since then. During the Turkish occupation from 1541–1686, for example, it was converted into the main mosque of the Turks. After the reconquest, it was turned over to the Jesuits, who refitted it in a Baroque style, replacing what had been carried off or thrown away by the Turks. The Jesuits also built a monastery and college on both sides. Over the years the church was struck by lightning and gutted by fire several times, so by the late 19th century it was not only a mixture of several architectural styles but badly damaged as well. At this time it was called the Coronation Church and also served as the main parish church of Buda; thus it was decided to completely renew the church. The work was led by the brilliant Hungarian architect Frigyes Schulek, who began by freeing the church from the crowding confines of the buildings added to it on both sides, and by removing the small additions. He then reconstructed it in the neo-Gothic style you can see today. The effect is truly awe-inspiring. The overall style is a unified Gothic; still, the elements from different ages incorporated into various parts of the building recall the important periods in the history of the church.

Let's take a closer look at the different features of the Matthias Church. The northern "Béla" tower and the main portal, for example, were reconstructed in the style of the middle of the 13th century, while the magnificent southwestern "Mátyás" tower was rebuilt in the Gothic style and was capped by a new imposing neo-Gothic steeple. The glazed tiles on the roof, on the other hand, were reconstructed from the design used in the 15th century. The valuable architectural elements which could be salvaged, such as the **Mary Portal** (Mária-kapu, southwest entrance) from 1370, were pieced together and put back in their original places. When you enter the church through the Mary Portal, you can also see the relief from 1370 above it depicting the death of the Virgin Mary. Only, approximately one half of the relief, the light-colored part, is original; the added parts, in keeping with modern practice in the science of preservation, have been tinted a darker brown to facilitate their differentiation.

The interior of the church was completely reconstructed in the late 1800's. The low vaults in the rear and the stairs at the entrance were reconstructed in the style of the 13th century, complete with a neo-Romanesque baptismal font on the right. The rest of the interior has preserved its late Gothic arrangement as a hall church with a main nave and two side aisles ever since the 14th century. Opulent painted decorations based on those found on remaining fragments of the original Gothic structure and further embellished cover the inside of the church. The design forms the frame for frescoes from the 19th century which, in addition to traditional scenes from the Bible, also depict the most important events in Hungarian history. The decorative patterns are the same throughout the church; still, in one place, two meters (6 feet) high on the southern wall, the straight lines are replaced by wavy ones, giving the impression that a curtain from the 150 year period when the Turks used the church as a mosque is still hanging there. This was indeed the place where a curtain was hung, behind which the women, who were not allowed inside, could watch the ceremony. On the upper part of the wall you can see stained glass windows from the 19th century which depict scenes from the lives of the

4

Virgin Mary and Hungarian saints Margaret and Elizabeth. These windows and the paintings on the walls were all the works of leading artists of their time (Károly Lotz, Bertalan Székely, etc.).

Neo-Gothic altars and decorations can be found in the side chapels and apse. The pulpit too, with the four Evangelists and the four Church Fathers on its rail and a statue of the Good Shepherd on its crown, dates back to the 19th century (designed by Frigyes Schulek).

The flags seen in the nave of the church represented the counties of Hungary at the crowning of Franz Joseph in 1867. It was for this occasion that Ferenc (Franz) Liszt composed the Coronation Mass. And it was to honor the Matthias Church that Zoltán Kodály composed the Buda-vári Te Deum, which was first performed here. The acoustics and organ of the church are outstanding even today, and many extremely popular concerts and masses with musical accompaniment are held here.

Museums beneath the church and in the oratory display both medieval and modern ecclesiastical objects such as reliquiaries and vestments. You can also see the coronation thrones and a red marble sarcophagus containing the bones found in the royal tombs of Székesfehérvár.

On leaving the church do take a minute to glance back at the imposing building and you will fully agree with the Hungarians in the early 1900s who so admired it that later when the lighting up of monuments came into fashion it became the first building to be lit up in 1928.

» On its completion as well, the magnificently reconstructed Matthias Church was marveled at by one and all, even by the architect himself. But behind it at that time there was only a crumbling wall on the outskirts of the Castle District with a narrow flight of stairs leading down the hill towards the Danube. The church deserved better than this, and by 1899 the Pest side had become so resplendent that it too required a counterpoint on the west bank. The idea was conceived to build a new bastion

behind the church complete with terraces from which the people could admire the magnificent new architectural achievements of Pest: the Parliament, the Basilica, the Promenade along the Danube, and the beautiful new bridges spanning the river.

5 Schulek had more than enough ideas left over to design the **Fishermen's Bastion** (Halászbástya) for the capital city of a country with a history of over 1,000 years. The Bastion got its name from the fact that in olden times this section of the Castle District was defended by the Fisherman's Guild. Its impressive stairways and terraces formed a splendid historical setting for the Matthias Church, and totally recreated this section of the Castle District. **‹‹**

›› Between the Fisherman's Bastion and the church you can see the **bronze equestrian statue** of the king who

founded the state of Hungary, **St. Stephen** (Szent István). The statue was unveiled in 1906. The base, decorated with reliefs of scenes from his life, was designed by Frigyes Schulek; the statue itself is the work of Alajos Stróbl. St. Stephen was the first king of Hungary (1001–1038), the direct descendent of a chieftain of the tribes which conquered Hungary, and the king who gained a foothold for Hungary in the western world. It was St. Stephen who converted the Hungarian people to Christianity, organized the country into administrative counties similar to those in western Europe, and forced the previously nomadic pagan Hungarian tribes to accept and conform to the evolving feudal Catholic state. He was canonized shortly after his death for his role in the conversion of the people. **«**

» Walking further along the Fisherman's Bastion you can marvel in the panoramic view of Pest. Then from the northernmost terrace you can look back at the **Hilton Hotel,** which, apart from being a modern hotel, encompasses numerous elements of historical interest and importance.

From the bastion you can see the remains of the Gothic nave of the Dominican Church of St. Nicholas from the 13th century and the apse from the 15th century between the wings of the hotel. Open-air concerts and theater performances are held each summer in this beautiful setting. Following the ancient walls, you will also see the remains of the monastery under the other wing, which housed a Dominican university. Thorough excavations were conducted on the site before construction began in the 70s, and the hotel was specially designed not to disturb the ruins discovered here. The central areas are built next to and overlooking the ruins, which lends a truly unique atmosphere to the otherwise completely modern hotel.

When you walk around to the front of the hotel, you will again be confronted with the past. The main facade incorporates the remains of a Jesuit college from the 18th century which was so severely damaged in World War II

that it was impossible to reconstruct completely. When the hotel was built, the old walls were left standing as a backdrop for the modern building. Further along you can see the rear wall of the tower of the church you saw on the other side with modern upper stories added. On the wall you can see a copy of the Bautzen monument of King Matthias which depicts him enthroned. In the modern church tower rising above the building you will find a casino. This was a daring idea indeed, and this casino is quite probably the only one in the world to be located in a former church tower. The hotel ends with a row of shops

6

from which a corridor leads to the cloister of the old monastery. Original stone fragments found here during the excavations can be seen on the walls.

The Hilton Hotel was designed by the Hungarian architect Béla Pintér. It opened in 1976, and has won international acclaim despite the disputable site chosen in the historical Castle District. ≪

The square in front of the Hilton Hotel was named for András Hess, the printer who set up the first printing shop in Hungary in 1473 in the building at **No. 4** across the square. The neo-Classical facade conceals many details from the Middle Ages. Inside the rooms on the ground floor

you can see the old vaults of the original building, which dates back to 1390. Today it houses a restaurant whose tavern in the cellar with its 600-year-old vaults and mold-encrusted walls exudes a special atmosphere to dine by.

In the center of the square stands a **statue of Pope Innocent XI,** who formed the United Christian League which, under the command of Charles of Lorraine, liberated Buda from the Turks in 1686. The statue of the Pope, the work of József Damkó, was erected on the 250th anniversary of this event in 1936.

Above the doorway to the building behind the statue you can see a small red ceramic hedgehog which has given the building its name. Around the turn of the 17th and 18th centuries several Gothic houses were combined to form this building. It served as an inn in 1760, but was most famous for being the site of the first theater performances in Buda.

>> Tárnok utca, the street we have been walking along so far, now branches off into two streets. Let's continue our walk in **Táncsics Mihály utca,** which offers a wide range of sights. The street begins in an impressive way with the beautiful Baroque palace from 1776 on the right hand side at **No. 1.** This building houses the main offices of the National Inspectorate of Historic Monuments (Országos Műemléki Felügyelőség Székháza). This institution is the central authority which provides theoretical and practical guidance in questions of preservation and restoration.

Continuing on, your glance will be drawn to the beautiful 18th century Baroque building of the "Erdődy Palace" at **No. 7.** Beethoven paid several visits to this building, which today houses the Institute of Musicology (Zenetudományi Intézet).

The building at **No. 9** stands on the approximate site of the original 13th century royal residence which was later moved to the new Royal Palace at the southern end of Castle Hill after its completion in the 14th century. Beside the former residence once stood the largest and most

7

important gate in the city, the **Saturday Gate** (Szombat kapu). It was surrounded by the homes of the Hungarian residents of Buda, whose weekly markets were held here.

The beginning of Táncsics Mihály utca formed the Jewish section of Buda in the 14th to 16th centuries. In the early 14th century, the overly zealous proselityzers of King Louis the Great had driven the Jews out of their homes near Dísz tér and out of the entire Castle District. Soon afterwards the king resettled them in this section of the town. Two synagogues, one of which was the main synagogue of the Jews, were built in the 14th century but fell into ruins and were forgotten. Only remains of the smaller one have been discovered; these can be seen in the building at **No. 26.** (Open: Tues–Fri 10–2; Sat, Sun 10–6 from May 1–Oct 31.) **«**

At the end of the street stands the **Vienna Gate** (Bécsi kapu), which was the large gate built in the 16th century to replace the Saturday Gate. As happened to all the gates in the city, this one was also destroyed in the 19th century when huge buildings were to be constructed in this area. Fortunately, neither enough money nor capacity was left over after the wave of construction on the Pest side to carry out the plan, and this beautiful historical area remained untouched. The Vienna Gate was rebuilt in 1936 for the 250th anniversary of the liberation of Hungary from the Turks. A monument was also erected for the occasion in front of it (Béla Ohman, 1936).

The square is bounded to the north by the 19th century building of the **National Archives** (Országos Levéltár). This building, which looms enormous in its surroundings, is a typical example of the errors in proportion made by architects in the 19th and 20th centuries. The atmosphere in the old sections of many European cities has been marred by buildings such as this.

However, if you stand with your back to the Archives, you will see one of the quaintest squares in the Castle District. This row of houses from the 18th and 19th centuries built in the Baroque, King Louis XVI, and neo-Classical styles presents a harmonious picture. All the houses are built to the same scale, yet all are unique. The small 19th century **Lutheran church** adds to the intimate charm of the square.

›› Opposite the gate to the city two narrow streets lead to Kapisztrán tér on the western side. This is a large open space where the **Church of St. Mary Magdalene** (Mária Magdolna-templom) stood until the Second World War. In medieval times the church served as the parish church of the Hungarian population of the Castle District, and during the Turkish occupation it was the only church left for Christian use. For 150 years Catholics and Protestants took turns holding masses and services here. Today the walls of the nave stand only knee-high, but the beautiful

tower has been fully reconstructed. It houses an exhibition of medieval stone fragments, and from the top the view of the Castle District is splendid. **‹‹**

On the other side of the square stands the building of the **Museum of Military History** (Hadtörténeti Múzeum) where **9** the children of Buda often play in innocent ignorance at games of war on cannons exhibited in front of the building. **››** Úri utca, the longest street in the Castle District, starts at the tower and is lined with innumerous beautiful historical buildings. There is not enough room in this book to talk about each and every one, so we will select only the most important. It is worth your while, though, to spend some **10** time looking at the beautiful facades and wandering into the picturesque inner **10** courtyards.

Perhaps the most important building in the street is the one with a deceivingly simple facade at **No. 37.** If you go into the inner courtyard, you can still see two stories of a medieval keep on the right-hand side.

A little bit further on, the facade of **No. 31** is very striking. One beside the other, you can see arched and bar framed Gothic windows. These two architectural forms are not so far removed in time; still, they probably represent two different periods in the history of the building (approx. 1440 and 1500). **‹‹**

>> After the next building a small street on your left connects Úri utca with the street running parallel to it, **Országház utca.** It's worth a few minutes' time to have a look at the courtyard of **No. 2,** where the ground floor retains numerous details from the Middle Ages which illustrate some of the **special features of the Castle District.** One interesting custom was that after the land was divided into plots, the houses were all built starting at the street line. Imagine that only the long wing on the left is standing. As the town became more built up and the families grew in size, an addition was built onto the rear of the lot in the direction of the town wall. Often later another wing was added on the second long side of the plot which was then connected to the first by a wing along the street side, spanning the entryway. Only a small courtyard remained in the middle of the plot onto which all the inner rooms opened. One of the most distinctive features of these buildings in the Castle District are the niches with seats (sedilia) found in the gateways which date from the 14th and 15th centuries. It is interesting to note that these niches were all walled over during the reconstruction of the 17th and 18th centuries and were quickly forgotten. Most of them were only rediscovered in the ruins after the bombings of World War II and presented a difficult problem for art historians, who were unsure of their function. Today it is commonly thought that those accompanying guests to the house and the servants of the house could sit in these richly decorated seats while waiting.

Another interesting feature is that almost every house has several levels of cellars underneath it. It used to be said that there were two Budas: "One on the top and one inside the hill." Over the centuries caves and passageways had formed naturally in the limestone of the hill which were later enlarged and added onto to be used as wine cellars and underground passageways. Well shafts were also dug down to the level of the water which seeped through the limestone layers, expanding the system even more.

Map 2

1. Castle Theater
2. Soldier's Memorial
3. Town Hall
4. Matthias Church
5. Fishermen's Bastion
6. Hilton Hotel
7. Vienna Gate
8. Church of St. Mary Magdalene
9. Museum of Military History
10. 31 Úri utca
11. Ruszwurm pastry shop

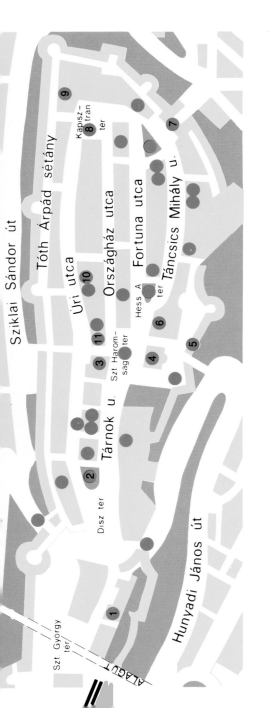

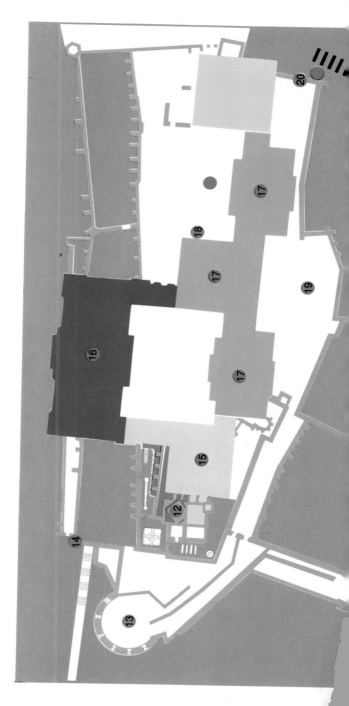

Map 3

12. Stephen Tower
13. Rondella
14. Mace Tower
15. Historical Museum of Budapest
16. National Széchényi Library
17. National Gallery
18. Matthias fountain
19. Statue of Eugen of Savoya
20. Neo-Baroque wrought-iron
    gates

By the late Middle Ages an entire system of underground passageways extended for several miles under the hill. This system was put to good use during times of war as the soldiers defending the hill could be quickly regrouped underground inside the castle walls and could be sent to the weakest point. In this way a mere handful of soldiers could give the impression of many.

By the 19th century these passageways had been forgotten and were not used by anyone, or rather hardly anyone, as they were rumored to be haunted and to be the hiding place of criminals.

Still, two brave young men in the 19th century realized the abandoned cellars would be the perfect place to grow mushrooms. They were granted a permit by the town council and, with their hearts pounding, entered the underground system of caves. They had just begun to relax and feel more at home and had just gotten started on their work, when they heard some strange noises. All of a sudden witches, ghosts, or some similarly suspicious creatures dashed out of the dark and fled through the passageways in a cloud of dust. The mushroom growers too bolted outside, only to realize by the cold clear light of day that they had surprised an officer of the cavalry who, in lieu of a better place, had arranged a tryst in the deserted caves with a hot-blooded maid from the palace. In their flight the young men left their mushrooms, the officer his sword, and the maid her velvet slippers as mementos for the ghosts who may truly have haunted the caves.

The underground system of caves proved extremely useful in the Second World War as well. The bomb shelters formed in the caves offered refuge to 13,000 people during the frequent air raids on the city. «

Today we can get a vague idea of what these passageways looked like in only a few wine cellars, and they too have been greatly changed. In a reconstructed section, however, a historical wax museum was opened a few years ago which brings to life shocking or exciting scenes from Hungarian history which are narrated in several languages. (Úri utca 9. Open: Tues–Sun 10–6.)

After looking at the building at **No. 2** Országház utca, you will find yourself again at Szentháromság tér. Now walk down the street opposite the church to the promenade along the western wall. On your way there, drop in at the quaint little **Ruszwurm pastry shop** (Ruszwurm Cukrászda) at **No. 7,** where you will be seated and served on the original furniture from 1827.

If you turn left at the end of the street onto **Tóth Árpád-sétány,** you can walk along the promenade back to our original starting points, Dísz tér and Szent György tér, while enjoying a panoramic view of the Buda Hills.

3. The Royal Palace

The southern end of Castle Hill is the site of the Royal Palace and its fortifications. In this area, which is somewhat separated from the civilian town, you can see the traces both above and below the ground of 600 years of construction. A short chronological tour of the palace and its eventful history will give us a general picture of the palace's past and lead to a better appreciation of the buildings of today as well.

Our story starts at the southern tip of Castle Hill in the beginning of the 14th century. If you walk from Dísz tér past the parking lot, across all the courtyards and through the lobby of the Historical Museum of Budapest (Budapesti Történeti Múzeum) **15** , you will arrive at a terrace overlooking the southernmost end of the hill. In the middle of the terrace you will see a few rows of stones of a slightly different color laid at an angle in a square and raised a few inches above the rest. This is all that remains of the **Stephen Tower** (István-torony) which the Anjou Prince

István started to build in 1330. (The Anjou Dynasty of Hungary: 1308–1387.)

Beside the tower, near where the terrace is today, stood a two-story palace with two long wings on either side of a V-shaped courtyard. Only a part of the wall of its chapel has survived and can be seen today on the Danube side of the tower. From here you can enjoy a beautiful view of the Danube, Gellért Hill and the Buda Hills, but the surrounding buildings and their history are equally interesting.

When construction on the palace had progressed sufficiently, the seat of the royal court of the Anjous was moved from Visegrád to Buda in 1355.

The first truly great period in the history of the Palace came during the reign of King Sigismund of Luxemburg

13

12—19

(Zsigmond, King of Hungary, 1387–1437, King of Bohemia, and Holy Roman Emperor 1433–1437). King Sigismund strove to improve the castle of Buda to a level befitting his rank. The majestic Gothic "Friss" Palace of King Sigismund far surpassed its predecessor from the Anjou period both in size and splendor. He also had a double system of walls built to protect the palace from the increasingly more widespread threat of cannons. He improved the southern fortifications by adding a **Rondella** (round bastion), a reconstruction of which you can see in front of you.

If you look around from the terrace, it is mainly the fortifications from the reign of **13** King Sigismund that you will see. To the right of the terrace you can see a section of the inner wall and, a bit farther **14** out, by the **Mace Tower** (Buzogány-torony) erected in the early 15th century, the outer wall of the castle which in the Middle Ages surrounded the entire hill, including the civilian town. The round bastion in front of you was part of a defense system which effectively guarded the gateway used by carts to enter the palace grounds. From the outer walls along the Danube a long wall-walk led up to the gate. The visitors had to pass through another corridor lined with high walls before reaching the gate in the inner wall of the castle. It was impossible for unwanted guests to sneak through so many guarded corridors. Additional precautions included a machicolated gallery on top of the bastion facing the hillside. From the reconstruction you can see that on the outside of the bastion a stone wall dotted with arrowslits protected the guards; on the inside only a wooden rail prevented them from falling off during a battle.

The fortress was even better fortified on the Danube side. Not only was there a double wall the whole length, but two huge curtain walls ending in giant water towers ran from the wall down to the Danube, cutting off the hill from an approach from the side. In one of the water towers there was an interesting structure built in 1416 by Hartman Steinpeck, the skilled craftsman from Nürnberg. He designed a horse-driven water pump to deliver water filtered out of the Danube, which was then still pure enough to drink, to the Palace.

>> After our look at the fortifications, let's go on to see the exhibit of the oldest remains of the palace on the lower level of the **Historical Museum of Budapest** (Budapesti Történeti Múzeum). On the floor below the entry level you can first see the exhibit of the coats of arms of the royal families who constructed the early buildings of the Royal Palace. After this you will go up and down stairs, passing through a labyrinth of narrow rooms lined with thick walls. These rooms formed the lower floor of the palace of King Sigismund. The original and reconstructed terra-cotta shaped bricks and stone fragments exhibited here recall the architectural elements and decorations of this Gothic palace from the late Middle Ages. The last two rooms are furnished with everyday objects—tableware, plates, glasses, jugs, majolica dishes, a tile stove, etc.—from the next era in Hungary's history, that of King Matthias (1458–1490).

On King Sigismund's death, following a brief period of internal struggle, Matthias was crowned king. It was during the 32 years of his reign that the country flourished as never before. In an age when the Renaissance was at its height, Hungary ranked with the best of Europe both in culture and politics. The leading scientists, philosophers and artists of the age lived and worked in the court of King Matthias, whose palace was made the marvel of all of Europe by the best artists and craftsmen of their time. His 2,500-volume library was one of the largest in the world and the splendor of his palace rivalled that of the Montefeltres' in Urbino and the Sforzas' in Milan.

We can only begin to imagine this magnificent Renaissance palace from the marble remains in the next room. Row upon row of fragments of window and door frames, fireplaces and fountains recall the most beautiful details of the Quattrocento period in Florence. Even so, a

15 great deal of imagination is needed to picture King Matthias' enormous palace, where every detail received the most careful attention and even the walls, ceilings and floors were all richly decorated.

Continuing on, you will reach the Gothic Hall of Knights from the age of King Sigismund. Gothic statues carved in graceful lines stand in rows around the room after having been found merely by chance in 1974 during excavations on the northwestern side of Castle Hill. The statues were probably left over after the reconstruction of the palace during Sigismund's reign, and were buried around 1430–1440. The discovery of the statues aroused great interest all over the world as they clearly reflect the influence of 14th century Burgundy, French Gothic sculpture. Isotope tests have shown that they were all completely painted and traces of paint can still be seen on some of them. The exhibit also shows other objects and architectural elements unearthed in the same area.

If you go from the Renaissance room through a corridor decorated with architectural stone fragments, you will reach the remains of the palace chapel. Built by King Louis the Great (Nagy Lajos) in 1366, the chapel originally had two stories, the smaller lower part of which is open to the public. The upper part, a much higher and longer church, was reconstructed by King Matthias in late Gothic style decorated with Renaissance furnishings and details. The chronicles of Hungarian history say that the chapel was so beautiful that the Turkish sultan Suleiman, who visited the city in 1526, wanted to take the entire palace and chapel back to Turkey with him. The upper part of the chapel was destroyed in the battles of the late 1600s. The 600-year-old walls of the lower story have been reconstructed partly in brick, incorporating the original remains whenever possible. The late 15th century winged altar (tryptich) from the National Gallery helps in part to restore the original atmosphere.

When you return to the staircase, you will see a small-scale model of the parts of the royal grounds which have been excavated to date. On the wall you can see illustrations of the Buda palace throughout the ages. You may notice that everything seems to have been sliced off in one plane on both the model and one of the illustrations above it. This leads us to the next major episode in the history of the palace. During the 150 years of Turkish occupation and the reconquest of the town, the palace buildings were so severely damaged that the Austrian engineers entrusted with the reconstruction in the 17th and 18th centuries

12—20

found it more efficient merely to tear everything down to knee-high level and to fill in all the areas with the debris to make the land level. They in effect "bulldozed" the land to make a flat site necessary for the building of the new Baroque palace. This explains why we talked about the ancient history of the palace in the "cellar"; that was the only place where the early remains could still be found and excavated. «

On leaving the museum, you will find yourself in the Maria Theresa courtyard. In the 18th century a U-shaped court d'honneur palace built by Charles III and Maria Theresa stood on the northwestern side to your right. This palace was later, in the 19th century, enlarged and remodelled into the enormous neo-Baroque building you can still see. The courtyard, however, has retained the beautiful uniform Baroque decoration to this very day.

16 Today the western wing in the back houses the **National Széchényi Library** (Országos Széchényi Könyvtár), which is the largest library in the country and the main collection center for all information pertaining to Hungary.

The wing facing the Danube houses the National Gallery (Nemzeti Galéria) **17** , and in the northern end you will find the Museum of the Hungarian Workers' Movement (Munkásmozgalmi Múzeum).

>> If you walk through the passageway guarded by lions carved in stone, you will find yourself in another courtyard. On the wall behind you you will see the **Matthias fountain** **18** (Mátyás-kút.) King Matthias, the great Hungarian Renaissance king, was not only a shrewd diplomat but also an extremely popular king whose name and deeds are remembered in Hungarian tales, songs and sayings. One of these beautiful romantic tales is depicted by this fountain, which was created by Alajos Stróbl in 1904.

According to the legend, King Matthias used to roam about the country in disguise. Once he went hunting in the forest with his men, and after a long day they happened upon the home of a hunter, who invited them to share his dinner. This was how King Matthias first set eyes on the hunter's daughter, the beautiful Ilonka, who was of course pure, gentle and irresistible. They immediately fell in love with each other, but when he left, King Matthias only told Ilonka to visit him if she went to Buda, still keeping his true identity a secret. Ilonka, deeply in love, soon made her way to Buda where she happened to arrive just when the king was returning in all his pomp and glory after a victorious battle. Ilonka, numb with shock, realized her beloved was the king, who of course hadn't noticed her in the crowd. She returned home, and believing her love to be hopeless, died of a broken heart. When King Matthias returned for Ilonka, he found only the empty house. (And this was how he came to marry Beatrice of Aragon...) On the fountain you can see King Matthias at the top, beautiful Ilonka to the right and Galeotto, the court historian, to the left. <<

In the middle of the courtyard, in front of the former stables, stands a statue by György Vastagh (1901) of a Hungarian horseman bridling his horse.

If you go past the fountain and through the passageway, you will see the main facade of the building and the large terrace overlooking the Danube. In the middle stands a **statue of Eugen of Savoya** (Savoyai Jenő), who was the commander of the United Christian League which fought to liberate Buda and the rest of Hungary from the Turks (József Róna, 1900).

From the terrace you will have a magnificent view of the Danube and Pest. The steep path leading up from the river between the old walls surrounding the city reaches the top of the hill just to your left. Beside it you will

19

see stairs and stunning **Neo-Baroque wrought-iron** **19**
gates which form the boundary between the palace **20**
grounds and the civilian town. Just outside the gate is the square where we started our walk, Szt. György tér.

Beside the gate on the side of the square nearest the river, you will see an enormous statue of an eagle. The statue refers to an important Hungarian legend in which a "Turul," a mythic bird resembling an eagle, begat the son of Emese, who was called Álmos. It was his son Árpád who led the Magyars in the conquest of Hungary. From then on the turul became a symbolic bird to the nomadic Magyar tribes.

» Behind the terrace is the main entrance to the **Hungar-** **17**

20

ian National Gallery (Magyar Nemzeti Galéria), which owns the largest collection of Hungarian art from the earliest period of the conquest of the country to the present day. The National Gallery was founded in 1957 and moved to its present location in 1973.

On the ground floor to the left of the main entrance you will find the collection of stone sculpture. The most outstanding pieces are the works of Giovanni Dalmata from the Renaissance period, which you can see in the first **21** room (**the relief of the profile of King Matthias and Beatrice,** and the Madonna from Diósgyőr). On the next floor you will find the collection of late Gothic tryptichs brought together from various churches throughout Hungary in the room on your right. These medieval altars with movable wings from the 15th and 16th centuries are deco-

21   21

rated with painted wooden statues and panels and carvings covered in gold leaf. Panel paintings from other altars are also exhibited in the first room. The most outstanding of these by far is the **The Visitation** (Vizitáció) by **Master** **M. S.** from 1506. The other rooms in this wing contain several works from the Baroque period which show a pronounced Austrian influence.

On the other side of the main staircase is the collection of 19th century Hungarian painting and sculpture. The best works from the historical paintings are those of Bertalan Székely, Viktor Madarász and Gyula Benczúr. The works of Pál Szinyei-Merse stand out from the rest of the collection. In his beautiful paintings (Picnic in May; Lark), Szinyei-Merse applied the techniques of impressionism long before its time. Separate rooms are devoted in the collection to the works of realist painter Mihály Munkácsy and László Paál, who was a follower of the Barbizon school of painting.

22

On the next landing in the staircase, you can see the huge paintings of Tivadar Csontváry-Kosztka. The vibrant colors and singular tone of his paintings set him apart from all the styles of his time. The next floor houses the museum's extensive collection of 20th century Hungarian painting and sculpture. The pictures of the followers of the Nagybánya school, who founded the Hungarian plein air style of painting, are exhibited on the right. The works of the leading painter of this genre, Károly Ferenczy, show a truly unique style.

On the floor below the dome, you will find Hungarian sculptures from the post-World War II period. The most gigantic of these at the top of the stairs is Tibor Szervátiusz's A Fiery Throne. This sculpture is dedicated to György Dózsa, who was burned alive on a throne of red hot iron with a fiery crown on his head after the crushing of the peasant uprising of 1514 that he led. Dózsa has since become the symbol of a people struggling against oppression. The other rooms on this floor are devoted to 20th century Hungarian painting, including works from all the most significant schools. Some of the most outstanding artists are: József Rippl-Rónai, János Vaszary, Adolf Fényes, Lajos Gulácsy, László Mednyánszky, Aladár Körösfői-Kriesch, Károly Kernstok, József Egry, István Csók, János Kmetty, Lajos Tihanyi, Róbert Berény, Sándor Bortnyik, Lajos Kassák, Béla Czóbel, Gyula Rudnay, Aurél Bernáth, István Szőnyi, Ödön Márffy, Gyula Derkovits, István Dési Huber, Jenő Barcsay, Lajos Vajda, Imre Ámos and Béla Kondor.

The works of important Hungarian sculptors from the 20th century are exhibited on the landings between floors (for example, Pál Pátzay and Ferenc Medgyessy). **‹‹**

Anno 1846

Váci Street
(lithograph by Sandman of water-color of R. Alt.)

IV. The Inner City

The boundaries of the Inner City of Budapest of today correspond more or less with those of the medieval town of Pest. A settlement has guarded the river crossing in this place continuously since the 10th century which slowly developed into a town, using the stones from the ruins of the old Roman fortress to build churches, homes and later the town wall. After the royal residence was relocated on Castle Hill, Pest declined in importance, but the town's hard-working tradesmen and craftsmen still formed a tight-knit community.

It was not until the beginning of the 19th century that Pest really began to flourish. This was the age when traces of a national consciousness began to emerge and the idea of forming the twin cities of the Danube into the focal point of the nation was conceived. The prosperity created by the Napoleonic wars also turned the people's thoughts to ideas of expansion. At this time the people's way of thinking was inspired by the Age of Enlightenment, and the arts were governed by the neo-Classical style. A uniquely Hungarian style of architecture also developed to meet the new needs of the age with clear forms and noble purity.

It was in this setting that the first plans for the systematic organization of the city of Pest were drafted in 1805. And by the 1860s the city had already been given a total face-lift in a homogeneous neo-Classical style. In the second half of the century and during the fervor around the turn of the century, the old town was not only enlarged, but unfortunately almost totally transformed. It was no longer merely systematically "organized," but was turned into a new metropolis of a completely different scale in which the old Inner City became just a quaint center of business and trade.

When the city walls were torn down, the Inner City was connected with the new areas of development. The narrow meandering streets were released from the confines of the walls, and a modern system of water and sewer pipes was laid. Huge new apartment houses, stores, cafes and hotels were built on lots whose price increased as rapidly as the city grew. In a few short decades the appearance of the Inner City was changed completely, and today it takes a tourist with a fine eye to catch the traces of the city of old.

In the middle of **Március 15. tér** (March 15 Square) you can see a section on a somewhat lower level than the rest which is called **The Pit** (Gödör) by the residents of Pest. Walking on down you will see the remains of a Roman fortress called **Contra-Aquincum,** which was first built at the end of the 2nd century and reconstructed at the end of the 3rd. This military camp was built on an area measuring 84×86 meters (276×282 feet), and was surrounded by walls more than 3 meters (10 feet) thick. The camp, part of the fortified border system built along the Danube, controlled the river crossing, and guarded the transcontinental trade routes which had passed through here since ancient times.

After the retreat of the Romans, the bridge they had erected soon fell into ruin. The walls of the fortress, however, were still standing in the 10th century when the Magyars settled down here. Over the centuries the traffic at the river crossing increased, and the trading post of Pest grew along with it.

>> On the other side of the square you can see the **Inner City Parish Church** (Belvárosi templom). While not the most beautiful church in Budapest, its mixture of styles from different ages does—like a small museum—paint a realistic picture of the changing circumstances of Hungarian history. Construction first began on a Romanesque parish church on this site beside an earlier cemetery in the

11th century. As was common practice in those days, stones from the ruins of the Roman fortress were used in the building. Along with the whole town, the church too was completely destroyed during the Mongol invasion in the 13th century. One small section of one wall remained standing, which you can see today incorporated in the wall of the northern tower.

As the size and importance of Buda gradually increased after the Mongol invasion, the traffic at the river crossing in Pest also grew. The town flourished, and so did the parish. In the 15th century a large Gothic church was built on the site of the original Romanesque one. The walls of the sanctuary and the side entrances date back to this period. During the Turkish occupation (1541–1686) the church was used as a mosque and was later severely damaged in the battles against the Turks. It was reconstructed in the 18th century in the Baroque style; still the Gothic buttresses and door-framings stand out clearly on the Baroque facades. At the end of the 19th century, the surrounding buildings were torn down to make way for the new Elizabeth Bridge (Erzsébet híd) **69** , leaving only this church untouched as a reminder of the past.

Every little detail of the interior of the church attests to the generosity of the patrons of different ages and illustrates the different periods in its history. From the 15th century, for example, you can see several windows from the late Gothic church on the wall of the sanctuary and the original tabernacle. Along the right-hand wall of the sanctuary you can also see a row of niches with seats (sedilia) from the same period, one of which used to be the Mihrab, the prayer niche in front of which the Turks prayed for 150 years. On both sides of the wall in front of the sanctuary you can see beautiful Renaissance tabernacles made of marble from the 16th century. Moving further along in time, the nave retains the Baroque arches and vaulting from the 18th century, and in the side chapels you can see the original Baroque altars. The loft above the entrance, the pulpit, and the tomb in the first chapel on the left date back to the 19th century. During the last major reconstruction at the end of the 19th century, the sanctuary was repainted with neo-Gothic decorations. In the last 100 years of the history of the church, only minor restoration work has been completed, including repairs made necessary by the Second World War. ◀◀

If you walk through a passageway behind the church which leads under the large buildings of the Eötvös Loránd Tudományegyetem (Loránd Eötvös University of Arts and Sciences), you will reach the shopping street of Váci utca. But before we mingle with the crowds in this pedestrian street, let's go a little out of our way to visit Felszabadulás tér (Liberation Square), a truly metropolitan square which is one of the most beautiful in all of Budapest.

At the end of the street an underground passageway leads to the other side of the bridge. Pictures of Pest from the turn of the century line the walls and are an unexpected delight. Very little of what you see in them can still be found today, but looking at them will help you appreciate how new the seemingly old buildings of the Inner City really are.

At the end of the passageway, take the stairs on the left and go straight up the street all the way to the Franciscan Church (Ferences templom) **25** , on the far side of **Felszabadulás tér.**

You are now standing in the heart of the Inner City where not even a trace of the scenes in the pictures is evident. Standing beside one of the busiest streets in Budapest, you would be hard put to imagine that 100 years ago this was tiny Hatvani utca, which only widened into a road outside the city limits. The city walls had already been torn down by then, and a network of majestic avenues and boulevards had replaced the old roads leading out of the city. This street, however, had remained narrow, dusty and provincial in spite of the busy traffic. Here, in the middle of the Inner City, the commercial center of Budapest, something badly needed to be done.

The final impetus was provided by the construction of the Elizabeth Bridge. A great debate arose over where it should be built and how. At one point it was even suggested that the Inner City Parish Church should be moved 100 yards out of the way. In the end it was decided that the small, run-down buildings surrounding the bridgehead should be torn down and replaced by a spacious modern square with roads leading onto the bridge from all directions. The Inner City Parish Church, one of the oldest historical buildings in Pest, was left untouched.

27

This was how the Elizabeth Bridge (Erzsébet híd) **69** , the square, and the imposing twin **Klotild Palaces** (Klotild-paloták) on either side of the street came to be built. These tall palaces, commissioned by Princess Klotild and designed as apartment buildings, were built in 1902 in an Eclectic style using mainly Spanish Baroque elements. **26**

The building of the **Savings Bank** (Takarékpénztár) next to the Klotild Palace borders the shopping district of Pest and the street level is a maze of passageways dotted with small shops and cafés. Built in 1911 according to the plans of Henrik Schmal, its facade is covered with colorful ceramic tiles and combines Venetian Gothic and Renaissance elements. **27**

≫ In the Felszabadulás tér of today, traces of the olden days can be seen only in the **Franciscan Church** (Ferences templom), which was built from 1727–1743 on the site **25**

25

28

of a Turkish mosque. The decoration of the facade and interior of the church have retained the original Baroque style. Outside, on the side of the church facing Kossuth Lajos utca, you will find a plaque made by Barnabás Holló in 1905 in memory of the disastrous flood of 1838. As it was placed at the height reached by the water, you can imagine the great damage and untold number of deaths caused by the flood. The bronze plaque commemorates the heroic efforts of Baron Miklós Wesselényi, who spent the entire night in a small boat saving the lives of countless drowning people. **‹‹**

28 In front of the church you can see the **Fountain of the**

Nereids (Nereidák kútja) from 1835. Starting at this square, a long road lined with stores stretches for several miles, continuing on out of the city to the east. This is one of the most important avenues in the city; along it you will find the main railway station in Budapest, the Eastern Railway Station (Keleti pályaudvar) 60 .

» If you cross the street by going through the underground passageway by the fountain and then turn left into Kígyó utca or go through the passageways in the building of the Savings Bank, you will find your way back to **Váci utca.**

This pedestrian street has been the most important shopping street in Budapest for a very long time. However, the past is only evident if you tear your eyes away from the store windows and look at the upper floors of the buildings. The buildings themselves are not all that old—they date back to the 19th and 20th centuries—but the street itself became important as early as the 18th century. Later it became a fashionable promenade where "the upper crust" would walk leisurely down the street at noon or in the evening hours. As this custom grew more fashionable, the prices in the stores rose accordingly. Soon only the most elegant stores could afford to open a shop here. Often the most celebrated artists of the day were commissioned to paint huge colorful signs which hung from intricate wrought iron brackets outside the well-known shops, and the latest fashions were modeled not only in the exclusive shops but by the stylish pedestrians strolling down Váci utca. **«**

Not only stores are needed to make a commercial center, hotels are also a necessity. Several hotels have been located in Váci utca since right after the Turkish occupation.

» At **No. 20,** for example, you can see the modern Taverna Hotel which stands on the site of the famous Nádor Hotel from the 19th century. It was named after Archduke Joseph of Austria, whose life-size statue stood above the entrance. (The word "nádor" refers to his position in Hungary as second in command after the Emperor.)

29

An interesting custom in those days was for inventors or innovators to rent a room in a hotel to display their products. Sartorius, the famous Viennese tinsmith, followed this custom and installed a rudimentary shower in his room at the Nádor Hotel. The contraption, extremely unusual at the time consisted of a tank and a hose hanging from the ceiling. By twisting and turning various handles and valves, the force of the water could be regulated from a fine mist, drops or splatter, to a steady shower.

After the Second World War only a small row of shops occupied this site until József Finta designed the interesting post-modern **Taverna Hotel,** which opened in 1985. **«** **»** At **No. 16** on the next corner you can see the building of the **Fontana shopping center,** which was built by György

Vedres from 1969–1984 on the site of a bombed out building. The special step-like design of the building created a charming square in front where after completion of the construction, the **Hermes fountain** (Hermész-kút) with its adventure-filled past was moved. Hermes, known in Latin as Mercury, was the messenger of the gods. (But even in this capacity it is a wonder how often he was able to warn someone of imminent demise.) Originally, the statue adorned the wall of the Merkur (Mercury) Bank, built in 1904. When the building was demolished to make way for the new Elizabeth Bridge, the statue was saved from being melted down in the last minute by a radio reporter and, as "conveying messages" is also the creed of the radio, it was set up in the radio complex. Fifteen years later when reconstruction on the complex was begun, the statue of Mercury was again in the way. After a lengthy dispute and restoration, it was moved to this place in Váci utca, and with its new base is now known as the Hermes fountain. **«**

» At **9 Váci utca** you can see the **Philantelia flower shop** which is the only place in the street where the original Art Nouveau style of the frame for the shopwindow and interior decoration has survived since the turn of the century. The house was built in 1840 in the neo-Classical style on the site of an old inn called the "Seven Prince-electors," which was one of the most famous of its kind in the 18th century. It boasted a huge banquet hall which could cater to 1,000 guests and which was frequented by members of the aristocracy. Concerts were often held in the banquet hall and Ferenc Liszt himself performed here at the age of 11. As an off-shoot of the neo-Classical style of the 19th century, which attempted to revive all possible elements from Antiquity, even Bacchanals were held here. **«**

» The next building at **No. 11/A** is called the **Thonet Building** (1888–1890). The colorful ceramic tiles from the famous Hungarian Zsolnai factory and the battlemented cornice make it the most interesting example of the Eclec-

tic style of architecture in the street. The building got its name from the fact that the Thonet firm in Vienna, who commissioned architects Gyula Pártos and Ödön Lechner, opened a shop on the main floor to display their famous bent-wood style furniture. **《**

At this point Váci utca runs into **Vörösmarty tér.** In the middle of the square you can see a statue of one of the greatest Hungarian poets, Mihály Vörösmarty (Ede Kallós and Ede Telcs, 1908). At the far end stands the **Gerbeaud Café** (Gerbeaud Cukrászda), which is one of the oldest and most famous cafés in Budapest. Its original 19th century furnishings invoke the atmosphere of an age long past.

31 31

Whatever time of day you visit it, Vörösmarty tér is always bustling. This is the first stop on the underground railway (see page **78**), people pass by it on their way to and from the nearby Vigadó Concert Hall, this is where the shops begin, and streets lead from here to the row of hotels along the Danube. People pass the square both coming and going, and if the weather permits, they often spend a few minutes relaxing here. From the outdoor tables at the Gerbeaud

Café or just from a bench in the square, you can listen to various street singers, watch magicians performing in the street, run into friends or acquaintances, or simply chat with other tourists. But with the onset of winter, the scene in the square changes drastically. The people watching from inside the heated café witness a much different scene. The statue is wrapped up in canvas to protect it from pollution and freezing temperatures, the street singers have disappeared, and the people hurry across the square bundled up in heavy winter coats. The hubbub of life has moved indoors into the stores and coffee houses.

On the right-hand side of the square you will find the **Luxus Department Store** (Luxus Áruház), which was built in 1911 by Flóris Korb and Kálmán Giergl. This building is a good example of the reinforced concrete structure and modern functional approach to architecture new at the time. The department store occupies the bottom three stories of the building; apartments, the top four.

There are two ways to continue our walk from Vörösmarty tér. We could make a small detour by walking straight ahead to Roosevelt tér and return along the Danube, or we could take one of the small side-streets across the square from the department store which will lead straight to the **Vigadó** concert hall 34 .

» If you choose the long way around, take the small street to the left of the Gerbeaud Café up to **Roosevelt tér.** This square, which used to be the place where goods were unloaded from the ships on the Danube, was lined with smaller buildings of a uniform neo-Classical style. One reminder of this is the **Tänzer building** at 3 Akadémia utca, a small street to the right of the Hungarian Academy of Sciences (Magyar Tudományos Akadémia). Later when the Chain Bridge, the first permanent bridge in Budapest, was built the square became an important intersection in Pest, and the market was moved out of the rapidly developing Inner City.

In 1867 this square was the site of a moving event. It was here that the Austrian Monarch Franz Joseph, after being crowned King of Hungary in the Matthias Church, pledged his allegiance to the country in a symbolic ceremony. Each county and city in Hungary sent a cubic foot of soil from a historic place within its boundaries, which formed a small mound in the center of the square. Franz Joseph stood on the mound and, pointing the sword of St. Stephen, the first king of Hungary, in the four cardinal points, vowed to protect the country from enemies approaching from any direction. When the traffic was rerouted in the square in 1877 the mound was leveled off. The trees growing here today can still be said to be rooted in the soil amassed in this square for this memorable occasion more than a hundred years ago. **«**

» On the northern side of the square you can see the neo-Renaissance building housing the **Hungarian Academy of Sciences** (Magyar Tudományos Akadémia). After an open competition, a lengthy selection process and debate, the plans of Ágost Stüler from Berlin were accepted and construction was carried out from 1862–1864. In addition to the vast collections of books, medieval codices and manuscripts of the Academy Library, the formerly secret archives containing documentation of innovations, collected between 1825 and 1950, also represents a rich source of material for research in the history of science. **«**

The impressive Art Nouveau building of the **Gresham Palace** (Gresham-palota, 1906) on Roosevelt tér directly opposite the bridge balances the massive Castle Hill and Tunnel at the other end of the bridge in Buda. Just a couple of buildings away from the Academy you will come to the boundary of the 19th century Inner City. Or if you look at it from the other way around, this is where the Inner City and the Promenade along the Danube begin. Before the Second World War the Promenade (Korzó) was a popular place for a leisurely walk. A row of hotels faced the Danube and there were always crowds of people milling around in

front of them. But for years after the war, the Promenade was a dark and deserted street, with only the sound of an occasional tram breaking the silence. Later in the 1970s when international hotel chains decided to build in Hungary, the obvious choice for a site was the bank of the Danube River. In a few short years the Promenade came to life again and Hungarians and foreigners once more stroll along the mall day and night every season of the year, enjoying the magnificent view of Buda.

>> The facade of the **Vigadó concert hall** faces the Promenade. This is one of the largest concert halls in Budapest, with a small theater, restaurant, night club and exhibition rooms all under one roof. The present building was constructed from 1859−1864 by Frigyes Feszl in a Hungarian Romantic style. It was built on the site of the old Vigadó,

34

which had been severely damaged in the 1848-1849 War of Independence. In the more relaxed years following the suppression of the uprising, not only politicians and writers, but artists and actors and actresses as well all endeavored to create something original, something truly Hungarian. The architect, who had grown up on the changing waves of international styles, strove to arrange his collection of architectural elements in a Hungarian way. When placed side by side on this Romantic palace, these decorations can be symbolically related to Hungarian history, at the same time creating an interesting, beautiful and unique style of architecture. **≪**

If you continue to walk along the bank of the river, you will return to our starting point, the Inner City Parish Church **24** .

But before we leave this area, there are several other buildings left out of our walk which deserve to be viewed. **≫** At the corner of Eötvös Loránd utca and Egyetem tér, for example, you will find the **University Church** (Egyetemi templom). This is one of the most magnificent Baroque churches in all of Budapest. It was built from 1722-1742 for the monastic order of St. Paul, which was founded in the 13th century by the recluse Özséb the Content (Boldog Özséb). This order, the only Catholic order of Hungarian origin, which was dissolved in 1949, was especially renowned for its craftsmen. In the 18th century the Paulines were so skilled at the art of woodcarving, for example, that they were the ones who made the most magnificent furnishings for the ecclesiastical buildings in Hungary. Exquisite examples of their woodcarvings can be seen in the pulpit, the pews, the doors of the choir, and the main portal of the University Church.

The church is harmoniously arranged into a nave and side chapels and shows a well-balanced space effect. The frescoes on the ceiling and the altarpieces are the work of Austrian artist Johann Bergl and date back to the 18th century. Beside the church you can see the former Pauline monastery, which was reconstructed in the neo-Renaissance style in the 19th century. Today it houses the College of Theology (Hittudományi Akadémia). **≪**

≫ The U-shaped Baroque palace at **No. 16** Egyetem utca, called the **Károlyi Palace** (Károlyi-palota), was reconstructed in a neo-Classical style in 1832 by Viennese architect Anton Pius Riegl. The garden on the eastern side has been replaced by a playground and a small park, and the building itself is now home to the **Petőfi Literary Museum** (Petőfi Irodalmi Múzeum), which contains a collection of selected relics of Hungarian literature. **≪** **36**

≫ The building of the **Budapest City Council** (Fővárosi Tanács; 9–11 Városház utca) was designed by Fortunato di Prati and Anton Erhard Martinelli. It was built from 1716–1735, and was originally used as a home for disabled soldiers. An average of 2,000 veterans lived in the home, although it had a capacity of 16,000–17,000. (In those days this was the size of a medium-sized city). With shops, a canteen, a school and a chapel which seated 3,000 right on the premises, the residents had no need to stir from the home unless they wanted to. In 1784 the building was turned into a barracks by Joseph II and it has housed the City Council since 1894. **≪** **37**

On the other side of the square at **No. 7** you can see the beautiful neo-Classical building from the mid-19th century which was the Pest County Council.

≫ At **Martinelli tér** you will find the **Servite Church** (Szervita-templom), which was built in Baroque style from 1725–1732. **38**

On the other side of the square, you can see two interesting buildings from more recent times. Built in 1906, the Art Nouveau building at **No. 3,** for example, has a glass mosaic on the facade which depicts the "Glorification of Hungary."

The Rózsavölgyi building next door at **No. 5** has a record and music shop on the ground floor. Béla Lajta, one of the pioneers of Hungarian modern architecture in the early

20th century, designed the building in 1912. The sedately decorated facade reflects the function of the interior with lower ceilings and smaller windows in the upper stories where the three-storied shop is replaced by apartments. **«**

39 **»** The building at **2 Pesti Barnabás utca** is almost the only stunning example of secular Hungarian Baroque architecture in Pest to survive the centuries. András Mayerhoffer, one of the most famous Hungarian architects, designed it in 1755 for the Péterffy family, whose coat of arms can still be seen above the gateway. The building has been a restaurant (**Százéves**) since 1831, and even today it is one of the best in the Inner City. A red marble plaque beside the entrance marks the level of water reached in the great flood of 1838. **«**

Anno 1865

Plan of navigable canal in the place of today's Great
Boulevard
(Ferenc Reitter)

V. The Pest Side
Beyond the Inner City

In order to understand how Budapest developed, we must go back in time and imagine ourselves to be in the 1860s and 70s. The wave of revolutions which swept over Europe in 1848 has reached Hungary as well, and the country's uprising, which grew into a full-fledged war of independence against the Hapsburgs, is now over. The strict policies following the crushing of the war have been eased up after the Compromise of 1867, which transformed the Hapsburg Empire into a dual monarchy with two equal political centers in Vienna and Buda. A country of rapidly increasing potential, Hungary is now in desperate need of a capital city which will act as the nucleus of the nation, not just in theory but in reality as well. The Chain Bridge spans the Danube River, connecting the two cities of Pest and Buda. Buda, with its unique historical atmosphere, is home to the main government offices and institutions, while Pest is mired down alternately in dust or mud.

Over a century ago, Pest, with its winding streets, was crowded inside the city walls which separated it from the surrounding villages. The need for something new had begun to be recognized, and brilliant plans were drawn up one after the other not only to improve the old city but to lay the foundations for the true metropolis so fervently desired yet still not a reality. It was obvious that the capital of a nation could only be created if the winding narrow streets were replaced by clearly defined avenues. And the cramped shops had to be replaced by modern stores and entertainment facilities which would lure the people into the city.

The challenge was enormous: to make Pest into a modern metropolis in merely a few decades. To meet this challenge, the Council of Public Works was established in 1870, bringing together the most prominent and most competent men of the time. Their goal was incredibly ambitious. Just as Napoleon III and Haussmann had shaped the Paris of old into a sparklingly modern city, so did they intend to create a flourishing metropolis on the banks of the Danube.

The layout of the city had actually been determined by the course of history. The town of Pest had been built up along the Danube with a wall surrounding the city in a semi-circle to protect it from invaders. Gates in the wall opened to allow roads to enter from all directions. In time villages and later suburbs sprang up along these roads. By the middle of the 19th century the wall had actually come to be outdated as the range of firearms had long before surpassed the protective barrier formed by the wall and the sloping bank (glacis) on the outer side. In effect, the wall hindered the expansion of the city, and the time had come like in other European cities to tear it down. In its place, a boulevard was built in a semi-circle, opening up the city towards the surrounding areas. The roads radiating from it were made into avenues connecting the nearby settlements.

The work progressed rapidly. Construction of the inner boulevard and first avenues was soon followed by the creation of two new boulevards, and the buildings along the roads leading out of the city grew larger and larger. This was how the layout of the main roads was determined in a boulevard-avenue urban structure, and this in turn also decided the location of the new bridges to be built at either end of the semi-circular boulevards, connecting the road systems of both cities. While the flat land of Pest made planning relatively easy, the hills of Buda did not lend themselves to the building of semi-circular boulevards, but merely to connecting roads. To this day, the streets of

Budapest follow this system, oftentimes overcrowded from the rapid increase in traffic.

As mentioned above, the boulevards and avenues of Pest were built in the second half of the 19th century after the great periods in architecture had given way to Historicism, or the Eclectic period. In this style, instead of searching for new elements, the architects decorated the buildings with details borrowed from previous styles. Initially, they adhered to seemingly serious principles, later merely to established conventions, often with completely free mixing of such elements. On their buildings Classical gateways, small Gothic towers, and windows familiar from Renaissance and Baroque palaces smile down at us, completely forgetful of their origins. Overly strict critics of modern times have sometimes protested against this utilitarian use of the past. For the most part, however, Historicism is today appreciated in its own right, and the most outstanding examples of this period are ranked among the masterpieces of architecture. From our point of view, perhaps the most important thing is that today passers-by can delight in the harmonious ensemble of interesting and pleasant buildings all on the same scale yet all differently decorated with a wide variety of elements. Foreigners in Budapest will be reminded of other European cities where, discounting the relatively few original historical monuments, so much was built in this style. Just think of La Scala in Milan, the Opera House in Paris, Ringstrasse in Vienna and Ludwigstrasse in Munich. This is a style common to most large cities in Europe. What is unique to Pest is that the entire inner area of the city was built or rebuilt in a mere 50−60 years; and while elsewhere you may see a single boulevard, an avenue or a building, here you can see multitudes of buildings from this period, making Pest the most uniformly Eclectic city in Europe.

1. Népköztársaság útja–Városliget

(The City Park)

Work was begun on Népköztársaság útja, the first great radial avenue, in the 1870s. At that time the old Pest, the forerunner of today's Inner City, lay along the bank of the Danube. A few kilometers outside the city a forest served as a hunting ground and a new race course entertained the spectators. As a flourishing metropolis could not be built in a few years, the plan was to build at least a stately promenade to connect Pest and the forest, which was to be developed into a park for recreation and amusement.

What an incredibly bold idea: to plan a wide road leading off into nowhere, shouldering the responsibility for what was merely a hope for the future; to build a road leading from the booming, flourishing Inner City to a city park which was still in the planning; to construct imposing public and apartment buildings as well as mansions along the avenue which would enhance its attraction, and —upon construction—would make them mutually increase each other's beauty and value. Although it now seems an impossible task given the economic difficulties of the 1870s, all this was carried through by hard-headed and quick-witted Hungarians in a mere 20 years. The dynamic expansion of Pest was launched.

Now let's walk down Népköztársaság útja. Formerly called "Radial Avenue," it starts from the inner boulevard in the center of the city. The tall continuous row of apartment houses and public buildings with trees dotting the wide avenue gives us the impression of a large city. Most of the facades of the buildings display a collection of mainly neo-Renaissance ornamental elements from the Eclectic period at its best.

» At the first square you come to, for example, two enormous buildings stand apart from the continuous row of buildings. On the right you can see the beautiful home of

40

the **Ballet Institute** (Állami Balettintézet; 25 Népköztár-saság útja) with its French Renaissance details built in 1883 by Ödön Lechner and Gyula Pártos.

Opposite it at **No. 22** you can see the building of the **40** **Hungarian State Opera House** (Magyar Állami Operaház).

The story of how the Opera House came to be built here is an interesting one. In the 1880s a fund was established to build the Opera House, but no site had yet been chosen. The lot in Népköztársaság útja was owned by the People's Theater (Népszínház), which however lacked the funds necessary to build a theater. The problem showed no signs of being resolved until someone had a brainstorm. The

Map 4

23. "The Pit"—Contra-Aquincum
24. Inner City Parish Church
25. Franciscan Church
26. Klotild Palaces
27. Savings Bank
28. Fountain of the Nereids
29. 20 Váci utca—Taverna Hotel
30. 16 Váci utca—Fontana shopping center
31. Gerbeaud Café
32. Hungarian Academy of Sciences
33. Gresham Palace
34. Vigadó Concert Hall
35. University Church
36. Károlyi Palace
37. Budapest City Council
38. Servite Church
39. 2 Pesti Barnabás utca

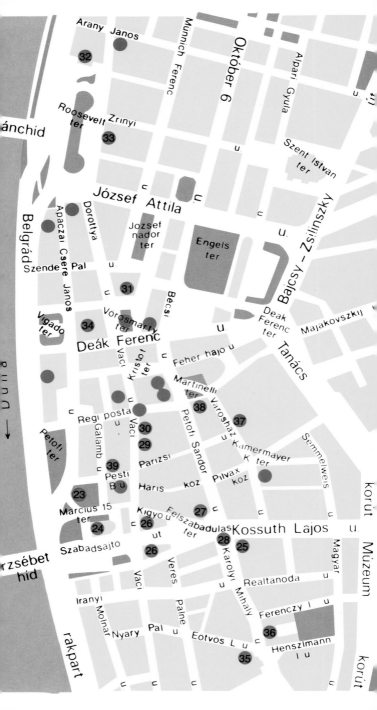

theater should sell the lot to the Opera House, which would have an affordable site and money left over to begin construction. The theater could then buy a cheaper plot of land and would still have enough money to start building a home of its own. This is exactly what happened, and in the course of a few short years, the nation gained both an opera house and a new theater.

An open competition was announced, various plans were submitted for the Opera House, and in the end the design of Miklós Ybl was selected. This magnificent neo-Renaissance building was built from 1875–1884 and meets the highest architectural and artistic standards. Not only was this one of the most impressive architectural achievements in Budapest, it was a work of art which could compete if not in size then at least in architectural merit with the European opera houses of the same period in Paris, Vienna or Dresden.

40

An arcade projecting over a drive forms the main entrance to the Opera House. Beside the drive you can see the statues of two great 19th century Hungarian composers, Ferenc Erkel and Ferenc (Franz) Liszt. Higher up you can find statues of other famous composers above the railing, and statues of the muses peer out of niches in the corners. This imposing facade hides a richly decorated interior as well. Its marble staircase, for example, is a true architectural work of art equal to the high social and artistic rank of the opera. In the rear of the horseshoe-shaped auditorium you can see the ornate box of honor; in the middle three-ton bronze chandeliers light the three-storied auditorium; and in the front the distinctive design of the proscenneum frames the stage. The interior decoration of the Opera House displays the talents of the leading Hungarian artists of the time (Mór Thán, Károly Lotz, Bertalan Székely).

Following the disastrous fire in the Vienna Ring Theater in 1881, the Budapest Opera House was the first in Europe to put into effect the internationally established strict fire code. Doors which opened to the outside, an iron curtain, iron doors and a sprinkler system to extinguish fires were installed by an Austrian firm.

Opening night was September 27, 1884. In the past one hundred years of its existence, the Opera House has played an important role in the highly recognized world of Hungarian music. In addition to the best Hungarian musicians, many famous foreign musicians have spent many years working here, including Gustav Mahler, Sergio Failoni and Otto Klemperer. The Opera House was restored to its original splendor in time for its 100th anniversary in 1984. **«**

Continuing on your way, you will see the **Divatcsarnok** (Hall of Fashion; 29 Népköztársaság útja) in the middle of the block on the right. The building has been a department store ever since the original Párizsi Nagyáruház (Paris Department Store) opened here in 1882. It was rebuilt in its present form in 1909 according to the plans of Gusztáv Petschacher.

In the next square you will see a **statue of Endre Ady** to the right and **one of Mór Jókai** to the left. Both are outstanding representatives of Hungarian literature, who are regrettably little known outside of Hungary. The square on the right hand side of the street is called **Liszt Ferenc**

tér, and in the middle you can see a modern **statue of Liszt.** The **Hungarian Academy of Music** (Liszt Ferenc **41** Zeneművészeti Főiskola, 1904–1907) stands at the far end of this square. Designed by Flóris Korb and Kálmán Giergl, it is an extremely interesting example of the Art Nouveau period in architecture. The Academy contains one of the largest concert halls in Budapest which boasts excellent acoustics, and houses the internationally acclaimed elite school of music.

At the end of the next block on Népköztársaság útja, you will reach a huge octagonal-shaped square. It was formerly called "Octagon Square" in reference to its shape, but today is known as November 7. tér. This is where Népköztársaság útja intersects the Great Boulevard (Nagykörút), the middle and most important boulevard in the street system of Pest. This is also one of the busiest streets both as regards traffic and shopping in all of Budapest. The Great Boulevard forms a semi-circle from the Margaret Bridge (Margit híd) to the Petőfi Bridge (Petőfi híd), connecting all the avenues and main roads leading out from the center of the city.

After November 7. tér the avenue takes on a new appearance. The rows of trees and the narrow service roads in front of the tall rows of buildings along them make the entire avenue seem airier and more spacious. In this section, the building on the right at **No. 67** deserves to be mentioned. It was built in a neo-Renaissance style from 1877–1879 according to the plans of Adolf Láng. From 1879 Ferenc Liszt (1811–1886) directed the Academy of Music, which he had founded in 1875, in this building until its present home off Népköztársaság útja was finished. A relief of Liszt can be seen on the facade.

The next building, **No. 69** (built 1875–1877), a former art gallery, today houses a Puppet Theater (Bábszínház). On the next corner the building with the facade decorated with sgraffito is home to the **Hungarian Academy of Fine Arts** **42** (Magyar Képzőművészeti Főiskola; 71 Népköztársaság útja). Built in 1876 as a school of decorative art, it became an academy a few years later when Hungarian artists who had been living and working abroad returned home at the request of the government to launch the teaching of the fine arts in Hungary.

At **No. 70** Népköztársaság útja on the left hand side of the street, you can find a pleasant café reminiscent of those at the turn of the century, **Lukács Cukrászda.**

» Soon you will reach another square, **Kodály körönd,** which was named after Zoltán Kodály (1882–1967), one of the most renowned composers of the 20th century. Kodály also conducted extensive research on Hungarian folk music and the teaching of music. He developed the world-famous Kodály Method of teaching music which many foreign teachers of music still visit Hungary to learn. Kodály lived in the building on the right (**87—89 Népköztársaság útja**), where a plaque can be seen in his memory.

The four statues standing in the middle of the square in the shade of hundred-year-old chestnut trees depict historical figures from the fights for independence of the 16th to 18th centuries (György Szondy, Miklós Zrínyi, Bálint Balassa and Bottyán Vak). **«**

After the square the avenue once again changes subtly. Nature is recalled not only by the trees lining it, but also by the small gardens in front of the buildings. And in the next block the gardens surrounding the mansions on either side of the street prepare us even more for the park at the end. Today the mansions in this area serve as embassies, offices and homes of the diplomatic corps, museums and apartments. While you enjoy looking at the beautiful buildings, just reflect for a moment on how well the plans for the development of the city were drawn up and what a subtle method was chosen to connect the city and the park. The avenue was divided into three parts, progressing gradually from the densely packed inner city to the airy spaciousness of the green park, so that by the time you reached the park, your mood would match the soothing, relaxed environment you would find there.

And now we come to the City Park (Városliget). These pleasant surroundings became a fashionable setting for the outdoor forms of social life at the turn of the century. ≫ Everyone who could went to the park by coach, on foot, or in a few short years on the **underground railway.** It was under Népköztársaság útja that the second underground railway was built in Europe, the first on the Continent. Even in the beginning it took this new "wonder of the city" only ten minutes to transport passengers from one end of the 3.7 kilometer (2.3 mile) route to the other. Inaugurated in 1896, the railway is still in use today. ≪

The **City Park** is the largest park in Budapest (about 1 square kilometer, 0.4 square miles), and the one with the most illustrious past. The forests covering this area were used by the Hungarian kings as a hunting ground from the 15th century on. In the late 18th century the swamps were drained and new species of trees were planted to create a place for the people of Budapest to go on outings. In the second half of the 19th century it was converted into a park for recreation and amusement using the most modern methods of landscape gardening. In 1896 the City Park was the site of the National Millenary Exhibition celebrating the 1,000th anniversary of the conquest of Hungary (the Magyar tribes arrived in the Carpathian Basin in 896). To commemorate the occasion, the imposing Millenary Monument was erected at the entrance to the park in Heroes' Square (Hősök tere).

≫ The **Millenary Monument** (Millenniumi emlékmű) **44** designed by architect Albert Schickedanz and sculptor György Zala, was built from 1896–1929. It consists of a 36 meter (118 feet) high column in the middle and a 85×25 meter (278×82 feet) semi-circular colonnade in two parts behind it. In the colonnade you can see the statues of the most important figures in the thousand year history of Hungary.

The seven equestrian statues in the middle portray the seven chieftains of the nomadic Magyar tribes who migrated from the east, conquering the Carpathian Basin in 896 and settling down here. On the top of the column, the statue of Archangel Gabriel, which was awarded the Grand Prize at the Paris World Exhibition in 1900, refers to the founding of the state of Hungary in the year 1001. Legend has it that Pope Sylvester II acted on the advice of the Archangel when he decided to send a holy crown to the first king of Hungary, St. Stephen, to legitimize the establishment of a Christian state.

The statues in the colonnade continue to illustrate the history of the state of Hungary as the allegorical statues of Labour and Welfare, War, Peace, Knowledge and Glory watch over. They portray the most important kings, military leaders and statesmen of the country, with the most important events of their lives depicted in the reliefs below. Of course, like every monument in the world, this one too fails to give an objective factual picture of history. Rather the mere selection of what was important and the interpretation of the events was determined by the viewpoint of the builders, simultaneously revealing an image of the ancient past and their contemporary present.

The first part of the colonnade includes two Hungarian kings who were later canonized, St. Stephen (Szt. István, 1001–1038) and St. Ladislas (Szt. László, 1077–1095), followed by King Coloman (Kálmán, 1095–1116), the creator of strict laws who is shown with his books, and Andrew II (II. András, 1205–1235), who took part in the crusades. This series confirms the fact that the first 250 years was a period of conversion to Christianity and organization for the new Hungarian state, which gradually won a place among the countries of Europe. This row of statues ends with King Béla IV (IV. Béla, 1235–1270), who survived the Mongol invasion and began to rebuild the ravished country. The next flourishing period, that of the Anjous is represented by the statues of King Charles

Robert (Károly Róbert, 1307–1342) and King Louis the Great (Nagy Lajos, 1342–1382), whose achievements in the reorganization and stabilization of the state were outstanding, and who greatly improved the country's foreign relations.

The right-hand part of the colonnade begins with the statue of Governor János Hunyadi (1446–1452), the great hero in the wars against the Turks. In 1456 Hunyadi defeated the Turks at Nándorfehérvár (today Belgrade, Yugoslavia), winning a respite for Western Europe which lasted 80 years. The leader of the country at that time was Hunyadi's son, Matthias (Mátyás, 1458–1490), who as we have already mentioned, ruled one of the most cultured courts of Europe and a strong, ambitious state in the Carpathian Basin. The reign of King Matthias could in every way be called the "Golden Age of Hungary." This period of prosperity ended with the Turkish conquest of Hungary. During the 150 years of Turkish rule, Hungary was divided into three parts, of which only Transylvania in the east enjoyed a relative degree of independence. The following three statues portray Transylvanian princes: István Bocskai (1605–1606), Gábor Bethlen (1613–1629) and Imre Thököly (1682–1685, 1690). Next in line comes Ferenc Rákóczi II (1703–1711), the leader of the fights against the Hapsburgs in the 18th century, and Lajos Kossuth (1848–1849), the most important leader in the Hungarian revolution of 1848—one of the wave of revolutions which swept over Europe in the middle of the 19th century—and head of the first independent government of Hungary formed during it.

In the original monument the last five statues portrayed Hapsburg emperors instead of the above mentioned. This gave the impression that after the decline of Hungary following the death of King Matthias the Hapsburgs represented the progressive force, first in the western part of the country when it was split into three parts during the Turkish occupation, and thereafter in the whole country when the Turks were driven out in 1686 and all of Hungary became a part of the Austrian Empire. The reliefs beneath the statues portrayed the emperors in the company of the Hungarian nobility in an attempt to legitimize their rule. The last of the emperors portrayed was Franz Joseph (1848–1916). During his reign Hungary began to prosper in the new Austro–Hungarian Monarchy formed after the Compromise of 1867, instilling hope in an even brighter future. If you think back over the thirty years preceding the Millennium, the rapid industrial and overall development seemed to justify this hope. This was the age of the regulation of the rivers, the construction of a network of roads and railroads, the beginning of industrial develop-

44

ment, not to mention the incredibly dynamic expansion of Budapest. It is little wonder then that a series of celebrations and a grand exhibition were arranged to display the achievements of history, and most importantly of recent years, which in this time of serious social tension, seemed to justify the role of the ruling class and gave new hope to everyone. The gateway to the exhibition was an enormous triumphal arch at the end of the avenue where the monument now stands. Beyond the arch, 240 pavilions were spread out over the 548,000 square meter (135 acre) territory which exhibited every Hungarian achievement in culture, the arts and business and was visited by almost 6 million people.

It may still seem incomprehensible that this magnificent monument was changed, but the explanation can again be

44

found in history. After World War II Hungary entered an era characterized by different goals and a different interpretation of history. The old interpretation did not fit in with the new philosophy, which held that the 400 years since the fall of Hungary to the Turks was a period in which the Hungarian people struggled for their independence against the Turks and, foremost of all, against the Hapsburgs. The benificient aspects of the ruling classes were not recognized, and the emphasis was placed instead on the struggle. The statues of the emperors were replaced by those of the princes of Transylvania who struggled to retain their relative independence during the Turkish occupation, and those of two leaders in the Hungarian fights for independence. The reliefs below depict them standing surrounded by the people. Ready at last, this seemingly ancient monument radiated a new message. **<<**

>> While the Millenary Monument was being built, museums were also erected on either side of it. The **Art** **45** **Gallery** (Műcsarnok) on the right (1895) was designed by Albert Schickedanz and Fülöp Herzog and today houses temporary exhibitions. The **Museum of Fine Arts** (Szép- **46** művészeti Múzeum) on the left (1900–1906), designed by the same architects, houses the largest collection of fine art in Hungary. The largest part of the collection of the Museum of Fine Arts came from the art collection of the Hungarian National Museum (est. 1802) and from the private Esterházy collection, which was returned from Vienna in 1870. Later, the works of Hungarian artists were transferred to the Hungarian National Gallery after it was

46

opened in 1957, leaving only the foreign works in the Museum of Fine Arts.

On the ground floor of the building you can see the small Greek and Roman Collection and the Egyptian Exhibition on the right. Behind this is the Collection of Modern Sculpture. The most outstanding pieces in this department are few small works by Maillol and a Rodin's marble statue. The rooms at the back show temporary exhibitions from the museum's large collection of prints and drawings. Temporary exhibitions from the collections of other museums are held in the rooms on the left and in the main lobby of the museum.

The Gallery of Old Masters, the most valuable collection in the museum, can be seen one floor up. On the right you will find works by Italian, Dutch and Flemish painters from the 13th to 18th centuries. On the left you can see the works of Spanish, German, Austrian, French and English painters. The most outstanding works in the collection are: Room 5: the works of Titian, Tintoretto and Veronese, as well as the portrait of Antonio Broccardo by Giorgione. In the smaller room off of Room 6 you can see Raphael's Portrait of a Young Man and Esterházy Madonna. In Room 9 and the smaller room off it you can see several paintings by both Pieter Brueghel the Elder and his son. Works by Flemish and Dutch artists fill Rooms 10 and 11 too, including several exquisite works by Rembrandt. The smaller rooms display numerous works representative of Dutch and Flemish landscape and genre-painting. On the left-hand side of the floor you can view the world-famous collection of Spanish paintings, renowned not only for its size but for its high artistic standard. In Room 15, for example, you can see seven extremely valuable paintings by El Greco; in Room 16, works by Ribera and Murillo; and in Room 17, the works of Goya and Velazquez's Peasants Having a Meal. The Austrian and German collection on this floor also contains numerous outstanding works: paintings by Lucas Cranach the Elder, Dürer's Portrait of a Young

Man in Room 19, and the exquisite sketches by F. A. Maulbertsch and the works of Paul Troger in Room 21. In the next rooms English painting is represented by a few works of Hogarth and Constable. The French collection is somewhat larger with important works by Delacroix, Corot and Courbet. The development of modern French painting is well illustrated by the works of Manet, Monet, Renoir, Sisley, Pissarro, Cézanne, Toulouse-Lautrec and others.

On the next floor the Collection of Old Sculpture exhibits outstanding examples of European schools from the 4th to the 18th century. **«**

Behind Heroes' Square lies the vast **City Park** (Városliget). The main sights to see are located along a road near the edge, while in the middle of the park you can find playgrounds, playing fields, lanes, and various gardens (Botanical Garden, Garden for the Blind...).

» If you turn to the left and walk along the road past the Museum of Fine Arts, you will first come across the **Gundel Restaurant,** which was built at the beginning of the 20th century. The restaurant and its garden have since become well-known all over the world. **«**

» Beside the restaurant sculpted elephants decorate the Art Nouveau entrance to the **Zoo and Botanical Gardens** (Fővárosi Állat- és Növénykert), which were established in 1865. In addition to the 500 animal and 1,500 plant species to be seen, the buildings themselves are extremely interesting. The steel structure of the Palm House, for example, was designed by the Eiffel Studio in Paris in 1917, and most of the other buildings were designed in a unique Hungarian style by Károly Kós and Dezső Zrumeczky (1909–1910). If you look carefully you will even discover amusing scenes in the wrought iron fence. **«**

» Walking along the road, you will next come to the **Circus** (Fővárosi Nagycirkusz) and the **Amusement Park** (Vidám Park) on the left. The imposing Eclectic building on the right belongs to the **Széchenyi Baths** (Széchenyi Gyógy- és Strandfürdő, 1909–1913). Originally, the water for the

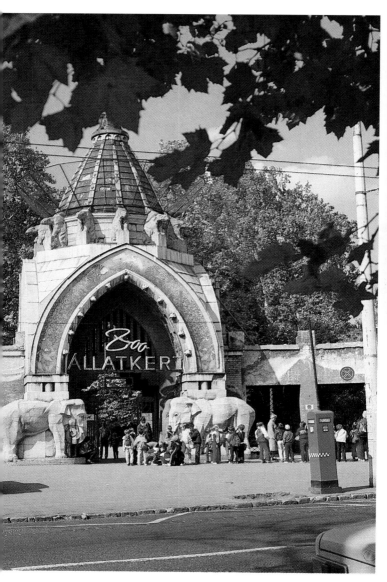

49

baths came from the 924 meter (3,031 feet) deep artesian well dug by Vilmos Zsigmondy from 1868–1878 but since 1936 it has come from a depth of 1,250 meters (4,100 feet). The water, which has a temperature of 76° Centigrade (169° F), is used in the treatment of rheumatism, neuritis and inflammation of the joints. Besides the medicinal baths, you will also find an outdoor swimming pool here, and those suffering from gastric disorders can "take the waters" in a small building in the park in front of the baths. «

» A little further along at 11 Városliget körút you will find the **Museum of Transport** (Közlekedési Múzeum). This **50**

51

museum has an extremely large and interesting collection of machines and means of transportation from all periods in the past and present. **《**

The bridge behind Heroes' Square crosses a small artificial lake filled with boats in the summer and ice-skaters in the winter. The building on the right contains changing rooms, a restaurant and service facilities.

》 On the other side of the bridge you will find the historical **51** buildings of **Vajdahunyad Castle** (Vajdahunyad vára) on a small island to your right. The idea of displaying the history of Hungarian architecture was conceived for the Millennium, and a temporary version of the Castle was constructed for the exhibition. To try it out, stand in the middle and starting at the entrance to the small chapel on your left, turn counter-clockwise. You will be able to follow all the major styles in architecture from the 11th to the 18th century starting from the Romanesque and Gothic to the Renaissance and Baroque. The architectural style of the 19th century is represented by the complex itself. This impressive display was created by combining exact copies of the elements scattered throughout Hungary which were most representative of each style. It was so successful that a permanent version was built of stone from 1904–1908. Today the castle houses the **Agricultural Museum** (Mezőgazdasági Múzeum). **≪**

2. The Boulevards and Avenues

After the building of Népköztársaság útja, work was begun on the boulevards. The Inner Boulevard was built on the site of the old city wall which had been torn down. What remains of the wall can still be seen in the courtyards of several buildings along the boulevard (for example at 21 Múzeum körút).

After lengthy deliberation, the next boulevard, the Great Boulevard, was routed along the path where a thousand years before a branch of the Danube had surrounded what was then the island of Pest. Over the centuries the river dried up and the river bed gradually filled up. Eventually all that was left was a small ditch running through the flat area bordering the walls of the town. As cheap water transport played a much larger role in transportation then than it does today, one plan suggested at the time was that a canal should be dug so that goods could be delivered from the Danube right to their destination. Bridges were to cross the canal at every avenue, and beautiful parks were to line both sides. This interesting plan fell through, and instead the ditch was filled in and the boulevard was laid on top of it. Water and sewer pipes were laid in the ditch as well as part of the widespread development of public utility works. On both sides of the street tall apartment houses were built in the fashionable Eclectic style described earlier.

After the two boulevards were completed, work began on the outer one, the Hungaria Boulevard, which was at that time located at the edge of the city.

Let's now take a closer look at the most interesting buildings along these main roads. We will only point out the most important ones along the way, as there is no room for or point in talking about each and every one.

52 ›› **The Lutheran church at Deák Square** (Deák téri evangélikus templom).

This Lutheran church, built from 1799–1808 by Mihály Pollack, is one of the first examples of puritan neo-Classical architecture in Hungary. The great architectural merits of this simple, undecorated building with clear masses lie in its well-balanced proportions and the true reflection of the function of the building in its design. The main facade was altered by József Hild in 1856, but the overall impression is still a homogeneous one. The high altar was designed by Pollack, and the altarpiece is a copy of Raphael's Transfiguration. The pulpit was designed by Ferenc Dunainszky. The excellent acoustics in this imposing hall church make it a favorite site for organ concerts. ‹‹

53 ›› The **Synagogue** (Zsinagóga, 2—8 Dohány utca). The Synagogue was built by the Viennese architect Ludwig Förster from 1854–1859 for the Budapest Jewish religious community of approximately 30,000 who lived primarily in this neighborhood. This Romantic style synagogue measures 53×27 meters (173×89 feet), stands 26 meters (85 feet) high, and has a nave and two side aisles supported by cast-iron pillars and arches, a structure strikingly new at that time. The walls are made of red and white bricks with ceramic decorations. Beautiful paintings and stained-glass windows adorn the interior of the synagogue, which has

room for 1,492 men on the main floor and 1,472 women in the two-storied gallery. The two towers with onion shaped domes on the main facade stand 64 meters (210 feet) high.

Beside the main building rows of arcades surround a mausoleum and cemetery dedicated to Jewish martyrs which were built from 1929—1931 in a style similar to that of the synagogue. This place is dedicated to the memory of the 10,000 Jews who died in World War I, and is the final resting place for thousands of Jews who died in the Jewish ghetto set up after the German occupation of Hungary in World War II. (During the last year of the war, approximately 450,000 Jews were the victims of deportations.) The **National Jewish Religious and Historical Collection** (Országos Zsidó Vallási és Történeti Gyűjtemény) can also be found behind the arcades at 2 Dohány utca (est. 1932. Open: Thurs 10—6, Tues, Wed, Fri, Sun 10—1 from May 1—Oct. 31). This institution plays an important role in the research on the history and culture of the Jewish people being conducted in Hungary. **‹‹**

54 **›› The National Museum of Hungary** (Magyar Nemzeti Múzeum, 14—16 Múzeum körút).

The building of the Hungarian National Museum was built by Mihály Pollack from 1836—1846 and is one of the finest examples of neo-Classical architecture in Hungary. It is one of the few neo-Classical buildings in the country which has retained its original function and in this way can be wholly appreciated for its functional and artistic merits. A majestic flight of steps leads up to the Corinthian columns of the portico of the main entrance. The allegorical figure of Pannonia, flanked by personifications of the Arts and Sciences, dominates the huge pediment.

Brochures describing the permanent collection in English and German can be bought in the vestibule of the museum. The rooms on the ground floor display the archeological remains of the peoples who inhabited the Carpathian Basin from prehistoric ages till the arrival of the

Magyars. The exhibits are described in both English and German.

Walking up two flights of stairs to the next floor, you will reach a domed hall decorated in marbled stucco. This is where the collection of jewelry from the 15th to the 18th century is displayed. In the rooms to the right you will find the collection of the history of Hungary dating from the Conquest of Hungary to 1849. Descriptions are provided in both English and Russian. Across from the staircase is the Collection of the Hungarian Royal Crown and Other Regalia. The most prized possession in the collection is the Hungarian royal crown, a closed crown which ranks among the highest types of medieval secular regalia. The crown consists of two parts which were subsequently joined together. The lower part, the "Greek crown," is a gold rim decorated with precious stones, pearls and cloisonné enamel plates with a top of "à jour" enamel. This part of the crown is presumed to have been made in the imperial workshops of the Byzantine Empire in the 11th century. The upper part, the "Latin crown," is decorated with embedded enamel plates and gold filigree. The exact details of the time and place the upper part was made and the circumstances of their joining are still disputed by experts. The coronation robe was made from a chasuble which was presented to the Church of the Virgin Mary in Székesfehérvár in 1301 by St. Stephen and his wife Queen Gizella. It is made of crimson-colored silk from Byzantium, and is richly embroidered with gold and silk threads depicting the Te Deum, the prayer of St. Ambrose. The other regalia are no less exquisite. The shape of the sceptre, for instance, resembles that of a typical eastern sceptre shaped like a mace used before the conquest. The head, 7 cm (2.8 in.) in diameter, is made of rock crystal and is presumably the work of craftsmen in Egypt in the 10th century. The richly decorated gold filigree setting was made at the end of the 12th century in the royal workshop of Hungary. The orb, with the double cross of Hungary on top, is made of gold-plated bronze and dates back to the 14th century. The sword, a replacement of an earlier one, was made in the 16th century by craftsmen in Venice.

On the top floor of the museum you can see the collection of the wide range of animal life found in Hungary. **≪**

55 **≫ Kálvin tér**

The simple Calvinist church and the buildings alongside it, all built in a neo-Classical style, form a harmonious ensemble in the center of the bustling city. **≪**

56 **≫** The **Central Market Hall** (Vásárcsarnok, 1−3 Tolbuhin körút). At the end of the 19th century when the open markets could no longer supply the needs of the growing city, construction was begun of five market halls more or less at the same time. The Central Market Hall (1889−1896) is the most beautiful and most interesting of them all. It was designed by Samu Pecz in a neo-Gothic style, but its modern iron structure, the logical arrangement of the interior, and the walls of plain brick, stone and terracotta preempt the functional approach of modern architecture. The 150 meter (500 feet) long nave is joined by 6 transepts on both sides. Originally the market hall had 1,100 stalls, was directly connected to the railroad, and was linked by an underground tunnel to the pier on the Danube. Today it is still a crowded bustling market which will give you a glimpse of the everyday lives of average Hungarians. **≪**

Nearby on the bank of the Danube stands the neo-Renaissance building of the former customs house built from 1871−1874 by Miklós Ybl. Today it houses the Karl Marx University of Economics (Marx Károly Közgazdaságtudományi Egyetem).

57 **≫** The **Western Railway Station** (Nyugati pályaudvar, Marx tér). The present Western Railway Station, designed by Ágost de Serres and Győző Bernardt to replace a smaller station, was built from 1874−1877 at the time the Great Boulevard was laid out. This impressive building with

57

its cast iron structure was one of the most beautiful and modern stations in all of Europe at the time. An interesting detail is that in order to ensure that the trains could still run on schedule, the new cast iron structure was built right around the old station, which was only torn down after the new hall was completed. **≪**

The first electric tram-line in the city ran in front of the station; opened in 1887, it extended to today's Majakovszkij utca.

≫ The New York Palace (New York-palota; today Hungária Restaurant and Café, 9–11 Lenin körút).

This building was built between 1891–95 to house the main offices of an American insurance company. With its majestic tower and ideal location right at the bend in the

5

119

Great Boulevard, it creates a marvellous townscape effect. The famous New York Restaurant and Café which once operated on its ground floor became a popular meeting place for leading Hungarian writers and artists in the early 1900s. The caricatures they drew of each other still line the walls of the restaurant, which was renamed Hungária in 1954. The interesting arrangement of the interior and the abundant Eclectic decorations make it one of the most impressive restaurants in Budapest today. **‹‹**

58

››Museum of Applied Arts (Iparművészeti Múzeum, 33–37 Üllői út). The Museum of Applied Arts was built by Ödön Lechner and Gyula Pártos from 1893–1896 in the special Art Nouveau style developed in Hungary at the turn of the century. In addition to the Art Nouveau and Oriental elements used elsewhere, Hungarian architects incorporated traditional Hungarian folk motifs in the designing of buildings in urban centers as well, founding a modern architectural style unique to Hungary. On this building as well you can see primarily Hungarian folk motifs on the ceramic tiles set in the outside brick walls, with similar ornamentation used in the interior. **‹‹**

Other outstanding examples of this special and fascinating style are: the Geological Institute (Földtani Intézet,

59

59

59

14 Népstadion út) built in 1898–1899, and the Postal Savings Bank (Posta Takarékpénztár, 4 Rosenberg házaspár utca) built in 1900.

≫ The **Eastern Railway Station** (Keleti pályaudvar, Baross tér).

The main station in Budapest, the neo-Renaissance Eastern Railway Station, was completed in 1884. Statues of James Watt and George Stephenson stand in the two niches on the facade. Its departure hall is decorated with the paintings of famous Hungarian artists Mór Than and

60

Károly Lotz. Most international trains arrive and depart from this station. ❮❮

And finally, a somewhat unusual line of thought, but one which deserves a few minutes of your time. While walking along the boulevards looking at the "grand sights," it is a good idea to peek into the dull, everyday buildings as well, or to wander off into a little side street which reveals even more about the time they were built in. We have already mentioned the period of Historicism, when new buildings were designed using the elements of past ages, often in a unique way, to create interesting and pleasant buildings which meet the highest artistic criteria. The "ordinary" apartment houses present the other side of Historicism. This period was "the art of decorating facades," which Adolf Loos, the famous Viennese architect who rebelled against the style, described as a "masked ball." The unsuspecting tourist is overwhelmed by the buildings dressed up in the costumes of Renaissance and Baroque palaces and can only try to imagine what high society gatherings must take place in the grand halls behind the facades. But if you walk inside, you will be confronted with an oddly uniform scene, the "barracks" of apartment buildings: inner courtyards surrounded by galleries with only one or two larger apartments facing the street and the rest small one-room apartments opening onto the outside gallery. In the tightly packed city, brick walls adjoin other brick walls, with the drabness relieved only by the occasional plants in the courtyard. Unfortunately, this too is one of the many faces of a city, one which may say more about everyday life and a given period than the "gold-plated" tourist attractions. Behind the spectacular sights of every large city you will find the more numerous but less glamorous and less interesting sights. And as one of the goals of traveling is to get to know a place, sometimes a few sober thoughts must be introduced into the picture to keep everything in proportion.

3. Government Offices

When construction of the boulevards and avenues was well under way and the downtown area of the city was fast being developed, there was still one area in the center of the city a little to the north of the Inner City from Arany János utca to the Great Boulevard which strangely enough remained untouched. The reason was the giant "Neugebäude" ("new building") complex. It was built as a barracks in 1805, was used as a prison after the defeat of the War of Independence, and was also the place where the first prime minister of Hungary, Count Lajos Batthyány, was executed. After the Compromise of 1867, plans were immediately drawn up to demolish the complex because of the bad memories, but it wasn't until 1897 that the plans were actually carried through. Government offices, for which there was a growing need with the increased independence from Austria, were located in this area according to an overall plan. Today this is one of the best-planned and most spacious areas in the city, with wide streets and a homogeneous ensemble of buildings all from around the turn of the century.

>> On the southern border of this area of the city, work had already begun in 1848 on St. Stephen's Church, better known as the **Basilica** (Bazilika), which was designed to **61** replace a small temporary church in the new town of Lipótváros just outside the city wall of Pest. The history of the Basilica was full of the unforeseen. Construction on the church was first interrupted by the War of Independence, and was only resumed in 1851. By 1867 the main structure of it had been finished when the architect, József Hild, passed away. Afterwards the uneven sinking of the supporting pillars caused the dome to collapse. The new architect, Miklós Ybl, continued the work, changing the earlier neo-Classical style to neo-Renaissance. Upon his death, the work was finally finished in 1905 by a third

architect, József Kauser, who left his mark by changing the decoration of the interior of the church.

The three different styles can easily be discerned today. The two side facades, for example, are built in a neo-Classical style, the front and back facades are in a neo-Renaissance style, while the interior has been decorated in a neo-Baroque style. In the middle of the tympanum between the two towers in the front an allegorical figure symbolizing Hungary can be seen, as well as statues of Hungarian saints. A bust of Hungary's first king, St. Stephen (Szent István, 1001–1038) can be seen above the main entrance, and on the door leaves you can see bronze reliefs of the twelve apostles.

The interior of the church is a Greek cross with additional corner rooms (cross in square) with a giant 96 meter (315 feet) high dome in the middle. In front of the supporting pillars stand the statues of Hungarian saints: St. Elizabeth (Erzsébet), St. Emeric (Imre), St. Gerard (Gellért), and St. Ladislas (László). A statue of St. Stephen carved of Car-rarra marble stands in the middle of the high altar with bronze reliefs depicting scenes from his life behind it in the apse. The most valuable painting in the church is the work of Gyula Benczúr, which can be seen on the altar in the southern transept. It illustrates the scene of St. Stephen offering his crown to the Virgin Mary before his death. Having no heir, St. Stephen asked the Virgin Mary to protect Hungary.

The Basilica is still an active Roman Catholic Church and is the largest in the city (area: 4147 square meters—44,641 square feet; length: 86 meters—282 feet; width: 55 meters—180 feet). Because of its proximity to the Danube, extremely deep foundations were required, and three stories of cellars were formed within them where the collection of the National Archives survived World War II.

St. Stephen's Church has been called the Basilica ever since it was built, although it is not arranged like a true basilica. In 1931 it was officially presented with the rank of "Basilica minor," legitimizing the use of the name. **«**

The old Neugebäude block included today's **Szabadság tér** (Liberty Square) and its vicinity. Two buildings both built at the same time in 1905 by Ignác Alpár can be seen on either side of the square: the **Stock Exchange Palace** **62** (Tőzsde-palota; today the central office of **Hungarian Television**—Magyar Televízió) and the **Austro–Hungarian Bank** **63** (Osztrák—Magyar Bank; today the main building of the **Hungarian National Bank**—Magyar Nemzeti Bank).

Do stop in the middle of the square and take a minute to compare these two impressive works of art. The buildings are completely different; still, they fit in well with each other and do not clash. This illustrates well the advantages of Historicism, the style which creates colorful townscapes composed of a mixture of different elements, yet the overall impact is one of a special harmony.

» A little to the north of here lies **Kossuth tér.** It is hard to imagine that this huge square (65,000 square meters, 700,000 square feet) was a mere field on the outskirts of the city barely a hundred years ago. The city was actually on the verge of using it as a land-fill when it was chosen to be the site of the **Hungarian Parliament** (Országház), the **64** largest building in Hungary (length: 265 meters—870 feet, width: 123 meters—405 feet; height: 95 meters—312 feet at the dome). It was built between the embankment and the square from 1885–1904 according to the plans of Imre Steindl in a typical Eclectic style. Its main arrangement comes from the Baroque style with a dome in the middle which enhances the beauty and elegantly emphasizes the noble symmetry of the building. The facade is covered on all sides with intricate Gothic arcades and tracery carved in stone, which makes it one of the most beautiful buildings in the city. Although the decoration is Gothic, it is not of a transcendental, soaring Gothic style. Rather it is made calmer, and more secure by the horizontal arrangement

64

which seems to exude faith in the reassuring power of democracy. The monumentality of the building and the world-redeeming mission of art are not reduced by the fact that shortly after the Parliament was opened two dozen policemen were forced to clear the building of the representatives of the opposition in 15 minutes after they had smashed the furnishings owing to a disagreement on political issues.

The main entrance with its three arches faces Kossuth tér and opens immediately onto a huge ornamental stairway leading up to the hall under the dome. The two completely symmetrical wings of the building were originally planned to house the lower and upper houses of the parliament. The outside roof line shows the placement of the two assembly halls which are used today as a Congress Hall and Assembly Hall. The two wings meet in the ceremonial hall under the dome which used to be the assembly hall for the two houses and which today is used for high-level state receptions. The Parliament Library (Országgyűlési Könyvtár), located on the side facing the Danube, is one of the largest libraries of social sciences in Hungary with a collection of 400,000 volumes. The leading artists of the time contributed to the interior decoration of the Parliament. Altogether 233 statues adorn the building, 88 of which can be seen on the facade. On the Danube side stand the statues of various Hungarian rulers from the seven tribal chieftains to Ferdinand V. On the facade facing the square you can see the statues of princes of Transylvania and famous military commanders.

Today the building houses the offices of the Presidential Council of Hungary, the Council of Ministers and the Parliament itself. **«**

In the square in front of the Parliament stand the statues of two great leaders in Hungary's wars of independence. On the left you can see the **equestrian statue of Ferenc Rákóczi II** (1703–1711) made by János Pásztor in 1935. In the middle of the group of statues on the right stands **Lajos Kossuth** (1848–1849) as depicted by Zsigmond Kisfaludi Stróbl (1952).

Opposite the Parliament on the left hand side of Kossuth tér you can find the former building of the Royal Supreme Court. Constructed from 1893–1896 by Alajos Hauszmann, it is now home to the **Ethnographic Museum** (Néprajzi Múzeum). To its right stands the building of the **Ministry of Food and Agriculture** (Mezőgazdasági és Élelmezésügyi Minisztérium), which was built by Gyula Bukovics from 1885–1886.

We have now come to the end of our walk through Pest and hope you have come to understand why Hungarians are so proud of their capital city. We have only shown you a few of the many architectural accomplishments and

65

130

merits of the period of Historicism which can be seen nowhere else in such great numbers. We hope that when you leave Hungary you will not only take with you beautiful memories of Budapest, but that perhaps you will look at similar buildings back home with a little more understanding and appreciation.

64

Anno 1761

View of Buda with the flying bridge
(engraving of J. F. Binder)

VI. Sights along the Danube

Budapest is built on the two banks of the Danube River. We have talked in length about the historical and commercial role the river has played, but we haven't even mentioned the fact that the Danube itself is what gives the city its special setting and enhances its beauty. The contrast between the two sides—the gently sloping hills and the flat plain separated by the serenely curving river—is a beautiful sight and a perfect natural setting for the city, which was

66, 67, 68

built to blend so harmoniously with it. This is why you mustn't leave Budapest without taking a boat trip on the river or at least a walk along its banks. You just haven't seen Budapest until you have done this.

Sightseeing tours by boat and boat excursions are offered during the summer, but if you do not have time or if the season is over, simply take a trip on tram. No. 2. This "panoramic tramline" runs along the Pest side of the Danube all the way from the Margaret Bridge (Margit híd) to the southern end of the city, offering you a scenic view of the river and all the sights along it.

As the river flows through different parts of the city, a homogeneous grouping of the sights is impossible. But we will describe all the sights we haven't discussed so far and you will find all the sights mentioned in this and other sections of the book numbered for easy reference on map **6.**

1. The Bridges

The river crossing on the Danube has played an important role throughout history. Since ancient times, transcontinental trade routes have passed through here, and in the Middle Ages, this was the point which connected the two halves of Hungary. Nevertheless, the need to be assured of fast, simple and safe transport across the river became a critical question only in the 19th century when the twin cities became increasingly dependent on each other, and crossing the river became a daily occurrence. This could only be ensured by a permanent bridge.

First, however, let's take a quick look at the many ingenious ways people had devised to get from one side of the river to the other. Late in the 2nd century the Romans built a permanent bridge on poles to be able to reach their fortress on the Pest side. This bridge later fell into ruin when the barbaric tribes who lived on a much lower level of civilization occupied the region. For 1,000 years to come only the ferry owners at the river crossing could help the people get to the other side of the Danube. During the reign of King Sigismund (Zsigmond, 1387–1437) and King Matthias (1458–1490), the idea of linking the twin cities together came up again, but only the first step was taken in this process when a pontoon bridge was built across the river at the end of the 15th century. In the 17th century the Turks built a similar bridge across the Danube which rested on 70 pontoons. Later in the 17th century after the reconquest of the city, the ingenious plan of an enterprising Viennese was carried out. A "flying bridge" was built which was a combination of a pontoon bridge and a ferry. The 7 meter (23 feet) mast of the boat was anchored in the riverbed. The ferry, which was 38 meters (124 feet) long with a 15×7 meter (49×23 feet) large deck, was attached to the mast by a long rope, which was kept out of the water by small boats. The river current enabled the ferry to move across the river and back like a pendulum using the rudder to steer it. In 1787 the last temporary bridge was built, which was a "Swaying Promenade" resting on 43 pontoons. 400 meters (1,300 feet) in length, 8 meters (26 feet) wide and covered with wooden planks, the bridge worked wonderfully for almost a hundred years. During the summer, that is. During the winter months the drifting ice-floes in the Danube made it necessary to dissemble the bridge, cutting off all ties between the two cities.

This is how it happened that in December of 1820 one of Hungary's wealthiest aristocrats received word that his father had died in Vienna and, stranded in the eastern half of the country, was prevented from crossing the river. As a result, the nobleman pledged a year's income for the construction of a permanent bridge across the Danube. It was finally built from 1842–1849, and was called the Chain Bridge. An exact reconstruction of it still spans the Danube today.

The aristocrat in question was Count István Széchenyi (1791–1860). In the course of his life he founded many institutions (including the Hungarian Academy of Sciences) and strove ceaselessly to develop his country. In recognition of his deeds he was already during his lifetime christened "The Greatest Hungarian."

66 ➤➤ As Hungary did not have much experience in building bridges, the **Chain Bridge** (Lánchíd; 1842–1849) was designed by two English engineers, Adam Clark and William Thierney Clark. A few years later Adam Clark built the **Tunnel** (Alagút) on the Buda end of the bridge to link up the growing areas of the city located behind Castle Hill (1853–1857; length: 350 meters—1,150 feet; width: 9.5 meters—31 feet; height: 10.6 meters—26–33 feet). Until 1918 a toll was charged to use the tunnel, as was customary in those days for both tunnels and bridges. ◀◀

67 ➤➤ The second bridge across the Danube was the **Margaret Bridge** (Margit híd), which was erected at the northern end of the Great Boulevard. It was constructed at the same time as the boulevard (1872–1876) by French engineer Ernest Gouin and his partner at the southern tip of Margaret Island and stretches 637.5 meters (2,092 feet) in length. In order for it to be at right angles to the current in the river, which splits in two to surround the island, the bridge had to be built with its two sections at a 150 degree angle. The side bridge connecting it to the island was built from 1899–1900 around the time the island was opened to the public. If you stand on the south side of the Margaret Bridge, you will have a spectacular view of the Danube and the two halves of the city. ◀◀

8 ➤➤ Two additional bridges built in the 1890s were named after Austrian monarch Franz Joseph and his wife Elizabeth. The first to be completed in 1894–1896 was the Franz Joseph Bridge—now called the **Liberty Bridge** (Szabadság híd). This 331 meter (1,086 feet) long iron bridge stands on two stone supporting pillars. It was designed by Hungarian engineers János Feketeházy, Aurél Czekelius and Virgil Nagy.

After this, construction began on the **Elizabeth Bridge** **69** (Erzsébet híd, 1897–1903), which did full justice to the beauty of its namesake. Its single span stretched for 290 meters (950 feet) across the Danube and until 1926 this suspension bridge was the largest chain bridge in the world. During the Second World War the Elizabeth Bridge was blown up, as were all the other bridges, by the retreating German troops. After the war, all the bridges except this one were reconstructed in their original form. The new Elizabeth Bridge (1961–1964) was redesigned in the modern form you see now by a team of engineers led by Pál Sávoly. It rests on the original pylons and remains a

69

suspension bridge with a single span of 290 meters (950 feet) supported by a modern cable structure. ≪

70 Much later, the **Petőfi Bridge** (Petőfi híd, 1933–1937) was erected at the southern end of the Great Boulevard, and the **Árpád Bridge** (Árpád híd, 1941–1950) was built at the northern tip of Margaret Island. Two railroad bridges complete the system of bridges in Budapest. The one on the northern edge of the city limits was originally built from 1893–1896 (reconstructed from 1952–1955), while the one to the south was built from 1873–1877 (reconstructed from 1948–1953).

2. Churches in the Víziváros

The Víziváros (Watertown) is an area which runs along the embankment of the Danube at the foot of Castle Hill between the Chain Bridge **66** and the Margaret Bridge **67** . The beautiful towers and spires of the many

4, 5, 72, 73

72

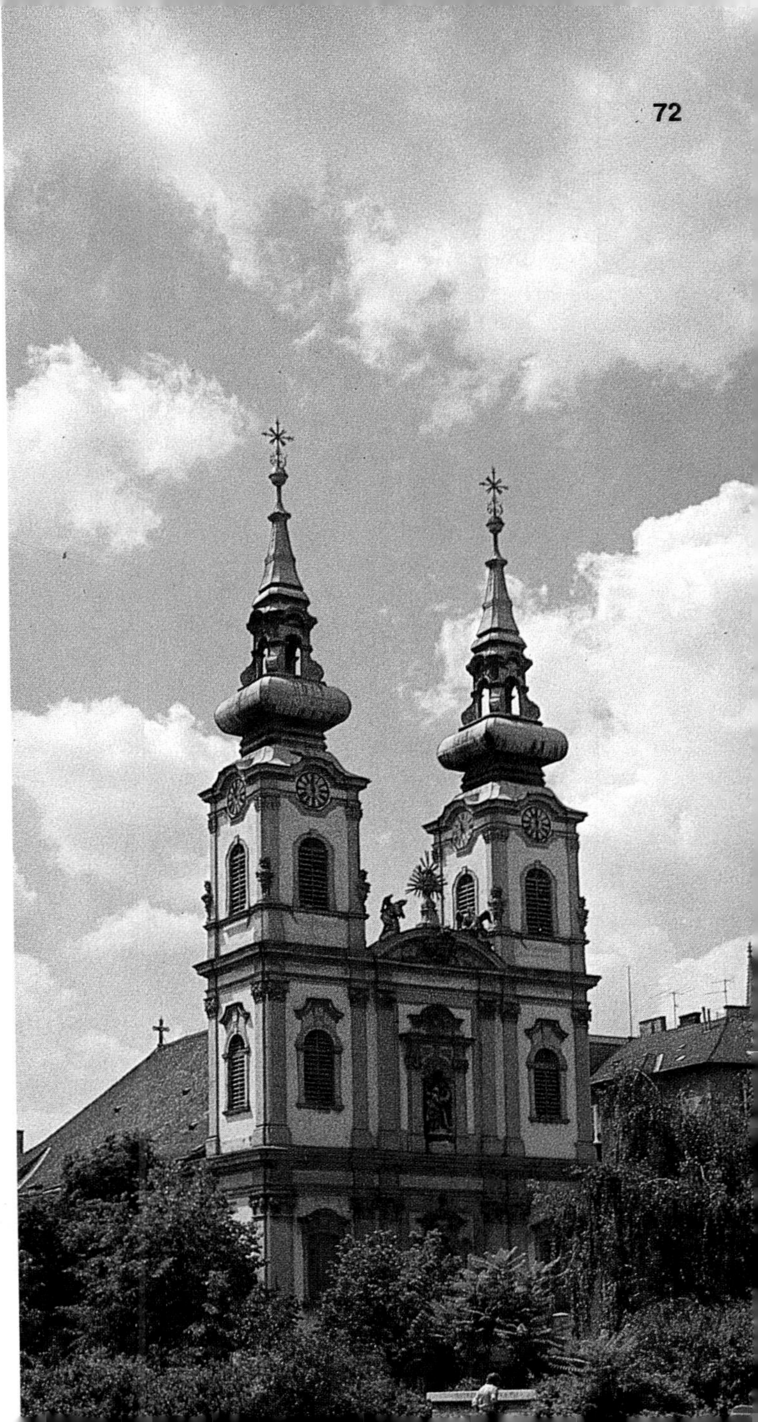

churches scattered throughout this small district of Buda direct your glance upwards from the river to the hill, almost as a precursor to the Fisherman's Bastion **5** and the Matthias Church **4** .

71 ≫ Starting from the north, the first church you encounter is the **Church of the Nuns of St. Elizabeth** (Erzsébet apácák temploma), which was built on the site of a Turkish mosque from 1731–1737. Wings to the right and left originally housed a home of refuge, a hospital and a convent. Built in the late 1700s, they were decorated with red and white elements from the late Baroque and Louis XVI styles. ≪

72 ≫ A little further to the south you can see the two towers of **St. Anne 's Church** (Szent Anna-templom). The church, along with the residence of the parish priest beside it, was built from 1740–1760 in the Baroque style, and its oval-shaped interior and dignified decoration make it one of the most graceful Baroque churches in Budapest. ≪

73 ≫ In the next square (Szilágyi Dezső tér) you will find a **Calvinist Church** (Kálvinista templom) built of red brick with a colorful ceramic tile roof. It was built in a neo-Gothic style between 1893–1896 by Samu Pecz. In the south-western corner of the square beside the church you can see a small fountain which the modest architect had decorated with a statue of himself. ≪

3. Medicinal Baths

Two different geographical features meet at the Danube: the hills of Buda and the beginning of the Great Plain in Pest. Where these two meet, a geological fault-line is formed and along a ten kilometer (6 mile) stretch thermal springs of various composition and with different properties break through to the surface. This beneficial feature of the area was recognized very early on by the peoples who settled down here. The Celtic tribes who inhabited the region in the first century named their city "Ak-Ink", meaning "abundant water." This name was later borrowed by the Romans, who called their city Aquincum. The Romans, who had long been familiar with the luxury of baths, built a veritable city of them. Fourteen baths from this period have been excavated in Óbuda alone.

The Magyars who settled here also quickly discovered the medicinal properties of the waters and took advantage of them. Curative hospitals renowned for their hydrotherapy were established as early as the 12th century in areas on the outskirts of the city where the thermal springs were especially abundant. One measure of how highly they were regarded is that even King Sigismund in the 15th century turned to them in hope of obtaining relief from his rheumatism. Those who recovered from their afflictions adorned the walls of the churches in the vicinity with votive offers of their gratitude, much like today the wall in the Lukács Baths (Lukács fürdő) **76** is covered with marble plaques inscribed with expressions of gratitude. The thermal springs were put to good use during the Turkish occupation as well, and the remains of the Turkish baths from this period are still some of the most colorful parts of our buildings today. After the Turks, the use of the baths declined greatly, and it was only in the mid-1800s that they regained their popularity again as the field of balneology became a science. Since then great efforts have been made to put this natural resource to efficient use. In Budapest alone 70 million liters (15 million gallons) of water pours out daily from 123 thermal springs and 400 mineral springs. Ten million people visit the 47 baths of Budapest each year, 70% of them in hope of a cure.

›› The most interesting baths in Budapest are the **King Baths** (Király fürdő), which were built by the Turkish pasha Sokoli Mustapha in 1570. The octagonal bath hall located under the large cupola in the middle is surrounded by blind arcades with ogee arches; the smaller halls to the side are

74

also covered with domes. All the wings except the neo-Classical one date back to the Turkish period. There are separate days in the steam baths and Turkish baths reserved for men and women. (Men: Mon, Wed, Fri; Women: Tue, Thurs, Sat.) **≪**

75 **≫** The square Turkish bath hall used at the **Rudas Baths** (Rudas fürdő) was also built by Sokoli Mustapha in 1566. The octagonal pool is covered by a hemispherical cupola decorated with colored glass windows. A vaulted corridor circles the main pool, and four pools with water of different temperatures can be found in the four corners of the hall. (This part is now a steam bath for men only.) The neo-Classical wing with the big swimming pool was added to the southern end of the building in the 19th century. **≪**

76 **≫** North of the Margaret Bridge lie the buildings of the **National Institute for Rheumatology and Physical Therapy** (Országos Reuma és Fizioterápiás Intézet, ORFI) and the **Lukács and Császár Baths** (Lukács és Császár fürdő). The curative powers of these waters, rich in hydrogen sulphide, were well-known to the Romans and to the Hungarians in the Middle Ages. During the Turkish occupation the springs were surrounded by mounds of earth, creating a small pond. The energy of the water bubbling up to the surface year round was used to drive a powder-mill and there was a small bath next to it. The mill pond (Malom-tó) still retains its ancient name, and the springs still bubble up through the bottom.

The new baths were added in the 19th century. The **Császár Baths** (Császár fürdő, 1841–1844) were designed by József Hild in a neo-Classical style although a bath hall from the Turkish period can still be seen in the building. The **Lukács Baths** (Lukács fürdő), built in 1924, include a swimming pool and famous medicinal and mud baths. These baths are both connected to the giant hospital, which was originally designed as a hotel overlooking the Danube. The most modern wing of the **hospital** was built between the two baths. The most advanced methods

and sophisticated equipment used in the science of balneotherapy are employed by the 150 doctors on the staff of the hospital to treat the 1,600 patients each year, many of whom are foreigners who come to Hungary especially to visit the hospital. «
» One of the most elegant thermal baths in Budapest can be found in the **Gellért Hotel and Baths**

77   **76–77**   **77**

(Gellért Szálló és Gyógyfürdő), which was built in 1918 by Artúr Sebestyén, Ármin Hegedűs and Izidor Sterk on the site of the medieval Medicinal Baths of St. Elizabeth. The baths in the magnificent Art Nouveau building can be reached either from the Danube side through the hotel or through the entrance on Kelenhegyi út which leads directly to the indoor and outdoor pools. ◀◀

4. Margitsziget (Margaret Island)

The most beautiful park in Budapest is Margitsziget (Margaret Island; see map **6**), which is situated in the middle of the Danube between the Margaret and Árpád Bridges. Originally three separate islands: Bathing Island, Painting Island and Rabbits' Island, it was surrounded by a concrete bank in the 19th century when the rivers of Hungary were regulated. The resulting size is 2.5 kilometers (1.5 miles) long, 500 meters (1,640 feet) wide, and an area of almost 100 hectares (247 acres).

The history of the islands stretches far into the past. They were already inhabited in Roman times, and are known from contemporary sources to have been a favorite hunting ground of the kings in the Middle Ages. In the 12th century various religious orders settled on the islands, which formed a virtual church state by the 13th century. When the Mongols invaded Hungary and defeated the royal forces, King Béla IV pledged out of desperation to send his daughter Margit to a convent if the country was saved. After the Mongols retreated, King Béla IV built a new Dominican convent on the island for his daughter, who lived here until her death at the age of 28. The island has borne her name ever since this time. When the Turks conquered Hungary in the 16th century, the convents and monasteries on the island were deserted and fell into disrepair. Only in the 19th century did it again gain impor-

Map 6

4. Matthias Church
14. Mace Tower
15. Historical Museum of Budapest
17. National Gallery
24. Inner City Parish Church
32. Hungarian Academy of Sciences
33. Gresham Palace
34. Vigadó Concert Hall
64. Parliament
65. Ethnographical Museum
66. Chain Bridge
67. Margaret Bridge
68. Liberty Bridge
69. Elizabeth Bridge
70. Árpád Bridge
71. Church of the Nuns of St. Elizabeth
72. St. Anne's Church
73. Calvinist church
74. King Baths
75. Rudas Baths
76. ORFI—Lukács and Császár Baths
77. Gellért Hotel and Baths
78. Termál and Ramada Hotels
85. Gellért Monument
86. Liberation Monument
87. Citadel

A. Japanese garden—Musical fountain
B. Tennis stadium
C. Water tower—Open-air theater
D. Palatinus swimming pool complex
E. Ruins of the Franciscan church and cloister
F. Fountain

70

Ⓐ
Ⓟ
78

Ⓑ

Ⓒ
Ⓓ

Ⓔ

Margit – sziget

Ⓕ

76
76

76

67

PEST

74
2

BUDA

71

Duna →

72

73

64 65

4

2

66

32

17

33

15

34

14

2

24

66

69

65 75

87 86 2 56

68

77

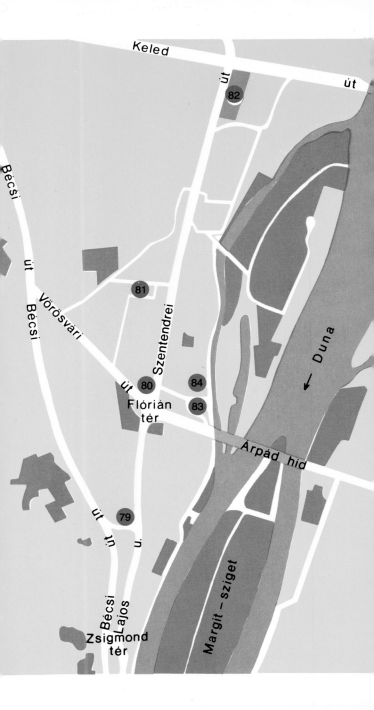

Map 7

79. Amphitheater of the Military Camp
80. Military Baths
81. Hercules-villa
82. Aquincum Museum and Archeological Site
83. Zichy Castle
84. Museum of Imre Varga

tance when it was turned into a public park and quickly became a favorite place for the residents of the city to visit.

The peace and quiet of the island is ensured by a law forbidding the use of cars. You can leave your car in the parking lot at the northern end of the island and traverse it in a mini bus, on a rented "family bicycle," or on foot.

The park includes many diverse features: lanes lined with 100-year-old chestnut trees, a Japanese garden, a rose garden, and even a tiny zoo. The ruins of ancient convents and monasteries add a little something extra to the mood of the park. The western side of the island has been developed for various sports, including one of the largest outdoor pools in Budapest, the Palatinus. During

the summer months, open-air theater, opera and ballet performances are held on the island featuring noted Hungarian and foreign guests.

On the northern end of Margaret Island you will find the **Termál** and **Ramada Hotels,** both of which have earned excellent international reputations for their combination of high standards as hotels and excellent results in the treatment of locomotor disorders using the thermal springs.

Anno 1911

Once typical house in Óbuda
(from the book of Albert Petrik on the architecture of old
Buda-Pest)

VII. Óbuda and Aquincum

Óbuda is the name of the section of Budapest which lies north of the Császár Baths **76** between the Buda hills and the Danube. This is where the Romans settled in the 1st century A.D. They named the region Aquincum, borrowing the Celtic name Ak-Ink, which meant "abundant water".

First of all, a military encampment was built in a square area 480×520 meters (1,600×1,700 feet) in size north of today's Árpád Bridge **70** . 6,000 soldiers were stationed in the camp, which was surrounded by a wall. A Canabae town grew up outside the camp with an additional population of 20,000 including the homes of administrators and public buildings. In time even a palace was built in the vicinity for the Roman Procurator. About 1 and a half kilometers (1 mile) to the north of the Árpád Bridge, a civilian town of 10,000 was built in a walled-in area measuring 380×460 meters (1,250×1,500 feet). All of these settlements were known collectively as Aquincum, which was the seat of the Procurator for the province of Pannonia Inferior.

Inside the walled-in areas, the streets were laid out systematically in a grid, but on the outskirts of the continuously expanding settlement the streets were allowed to run irregularly. The villas of the wealthy were built on the slopes of the hills, and farms were set up along the main roads outside the town. These cities represented the highest level of civilization reached by the Roman Empire. In magnificent baths fed by thermal springs, theaters and sports gymnasiums the inhabitants nursed their bodies and souls in accordance with the Roman motto "mens sana in corpore sano." A forum, a market hall and various public buildings were also erected in the city. And to protect the various flourishing cities, watch towers were built along the Danube, and two fortresses were constructed on the opposite side of the river to guard the limes, the boundary of the Empire.

Roman rule was crushed by barbarian tribes migrating from the east who lived on among the partially destroyed stone buildings. Legend has it that the famous king of the Huns, Attila, resided here as well in the 5th century. This assumption led Óbuda to be called Etzilburg, "Attila's castle" in German, until the 16th century. In the ancient German saga Nibelunglied it is even mentioned that this is where Attila and Krimhilda were wed. To this day it is not clear how much of the legend is true, but this is probably how the story that the Magyars were the descendents of the Huns came to spread in the Middle Ages. The Nibelunglied was written down in the 12th century and the historians of Frederick Barbarossa, Holy Roman Emperor, also told of his visiting Etzilburg. In their vivid account they describe Óbuda much as the legends did Attila's town. In the 12th century it was one of the most important settlements in the country. In the 13th century the increased role of Buda caused the secular importance of Óbuda to decline, but it became one of the strongholds of the church. This is why when in 1343 King Louis the Great gave the castle at Óbuda to his mother as the Queen's castle, even the king was made to pay a symbolic tax of one gold piece a year as proof of the church's authority. The intellectual and spiritual life of Óbuda flourished under the rule of the church. In 1389, for example, King Sigismund established Hungary's first—albeit short-lived—university in Óbuda. The economic prosperity of the city declined, however, and by the Middle Ages it had been reduced to an agricultural settlement of grape growers.

Jumping ahead in history, in the beginning of the 19th century, the trades and crafts in Óbuda began to prosper.

In 1870 the phyloxera blight destroyed the vines in the region, and factories were established around the town to provide work for the people. In 1873 Óbuda united with Buda, Pest and some surrounding towns to form the city of Budapest. Up until the Second World War, Óbuda was one of the most colorful sections of the new capital. The appearance and atmosphere of the old Baroque section of the inner area remained almost untouched and inspired countless writers and artists. The winding streets, humble houses and cheap cheerful neighborhood bars were famous before the war. Unfortunately, the battles of World War II destroyed a great percentage of the buildings, which were usually replaced by modern buildings. Still, the few traces of the past which have survived give us a feeling for the atmosphere of the city of old.

1. The Roman City

Historical records tell of the many peoples who settled on the ruins of the Roman city. Despite this, some parts of the old city have survived, usually 2–3 meters (5–10 feet) under the ground, the street level to the Romans. This is why we sometimes have to go down below the surface to view the ancient remains. In several cellars and underground passageways even museums can be found; in this small book we will mention only the most important ones.

>> **Amphitheater of the Military Camp** (Katonai tábor amfiteátruma; at the corner of Bécsi út and Nagyszombat utca)
This huge amphitheater, which measured 131×107 meters (430×351 feet), was built in the 2nd century and could accommodate 10,000–12,000 spectators. The arena (89×66 meters—291×216 feet) was surrounded by a 4 meter (13 feet) wall to protect the audience from the wild animals which were part of the battles. The people

who occupied the region after the Romans often used the amphitheater as part of their system of protective walls, and the chronicles of Hungarian history even tell of one tribal chieftain who built his castle among the ruins of the amphitheater after the conquest of Hungary. **«**

»Military Baths (Katonai város közfürdője; Underground passageway at Flórián tér)

In this unusual underground passageway you can see the remains of enormous public baths from the 1st to 2nd century which measured 120×140 meters (390×460 feet). The ancient Roman heating system has also been preserved in an excellent state here. **«**

»Hercules-villa (21 Meggyfa utca).

This is probably the area where the palaces of high-ranking administrators stood. In the protective structures of the museum, you can see just a part of one of these buildings. The villa was named after the mosaic on the floor in one of the rooms which depicts Hercules. Other exhibits include geometric mosaics and remains of wall paintings from the 2nd and 3rd centuries. **«**

»Aquincum Museum and Archeological Site (Polgár-város romterülete; 139 Szentendrei út).

The archeological site shows the remains of a budding civilian town from the 2nd to 3rd century. Similar to the Roman military camp, two streets passed straight through the city, crossing in the middle and leading in all four directions to a gate in the wall which surrounded the city. The walled-in area measured 380×520 meters (1,250×1,700 feet). The city center was situated at the intersection of the two roads; this is where the Forum, the Capitol Church, the Basilica (the court of law), the Curia (tribunal) and the large public baths were built. To the south shops lined the main road and a little further away stood a market hall and the Fortuna Augusta temple for the imperial cult. In the part of the city lying along the Danube and along the roads leading out of the city, excavations have uncovered the remains of five temples of the Mithras

cult and several Christian shrines from the 4th century. In the southeastern part of the archeological site you can see the bath of a private house with a large mosaic on the floor in relatively good condition. Rain and sewage canals ran under the entire city, and an aquaduct conducted water to the buildings in the civilian and military towns from springs five kilometers (3 miles) to the north. The original remains and a reconstructed section of the aquaduct can be seen along Szentendrei út. The baths were heated under the floors and clay pipes for heating were built into the walls as well.

Brochures in several languages are available at the entrance which provide maps and explanations of the ruins. In the museum you can see the drawings and the reconstructed plans of the buildings beside the unearthed objects. The floors will also help you to better understand the various parts of the site. The color red is used for inside halls, white for the covered outdoor halls, and the green grass represents the open areas. The red lines on the walls separates the original ruins from the reconstructions above. (Open: Tues–Sun 10–5 from May 1–Oct 31.) **《**

2. Óbuda

As we have already mentioned, very little of the old atmosphere of Óbuda has been preserved. However, the mainly Baroque buildings surrounding the old main square (Fő tér) were recently restored to their original beauty. Restaurants and museums now occupy these houses, which form a quaint "island" isolated among the tall modern buildings.

》 The eastern side of the square is bordered by the Baroque building of the **Zichy Castle** (Zichy-kastély, 1746–1757). Each summer concerts are held in its court-

83

yard, and the building itself houses the permanent collection of the **Lajos Kassák Memorial Museum** (Kassák Lajos Emlékmúzeum) and temporary exhibitions. Lajos Kassák (1887–1967) was a writer, poet, painter and expert on art. His most significant works were in the constructivist style. He also played an important role in the organization and popularization of avant-garde movements in Hungary. Since 1987 the Zichy Castle has also been the home of the permanent exhibition of **Victor Vasarely** (1908–), a world-famous painter of Hungarian origin and founder of the OP-ART style (entrance on Korvin Ottó tér). **«**

In the rest of the square you can see buildings of many colors with various restaurants and wine bars. The statues

84 of strollers holding umbrellas by **Imre Varga** (1923–) lead you to Laktanya utca, where you will find **Museum** of this renowned contemporary sculptor in the building at **No. 7.** The collection includes small and large works as well as models of his statues exhibited in public squares. (Open: Tues–Sun from 10–6.)

Anno 1835

View of Buda and Pest from the base of Gellért Hill
(etching of I. Weisenberg)

VIII. Gellért Hill—
Farewell to Budapest

The huge dolomite mass called Gellért Hill (Gellért-hegy) rose to its height of approximately 140 meters (460 feet) above the Danube in the last one million years. From the top you can enjoy a magnificent view of the entire city of Budapest.

>> The hill was named after Bishop Gellért (St. Gerard), who came to Hungary from Venice at the request of St. Stephen (István), the first king of Hungary, to assist in the conversion to Christianity of the largely pagan population. Legend has it that Bishop Gellért was captured during a

 85

85

pagan uprising in 1046, and was put into a barrel, which was then nailed shut and rolled off the hill into the Danube. The imposing **Gellért Monument** (Szt. Gellért-szobor) by Gyula Jankovics on the hillside opposite the Elizabeth Bridge was erected in 1904 in his memory. ‹‹

›› At the top of the hill you can see the **Liberation Monument** (Szabadság szobor) made by Zsigmond Kisfaludy Stróbl, which was erected in 1947 to commemorate the liberation of Hungary in World War II. The main figure is that of an enormous woman holding aloft a palm branch, the symbol of freedom. On her two sides you can see an allegorical figure symbolizing the struggle against destruction, the Dragonslayer, and the imposing figure of a man holding high a torch symbolizing progress. ‹‹

›› Behind the monument you will find the **Citadel** (Citadella), which was built in this strategic place by the Austrians after the crushing of the 1848–1849 War of Independence. Today it is a restaurant and a tourist hostel. Both from the terraces inside the fortress and alongside the walls outside you will have an unparalleled view of the city. ‹‹

We started to get to know Budapest from the far bank of

the Danube. Let's end our story here on top of the hill. From here, one beside the other, you can see the various parts of the city that we have explored bit by bit. We have become acquainted with the individual sights that in the end make up the complete picture and overall impression you will treasure in your memory.

A city is always much more than a mere collection of sights, and we hope that Budapest has unveiled its true self to you during our walk.

IX. Practical Information

We have tried to include in this last section some important information you might find useful during your stay in Budapest. An entire book could be written on the topic, but this is intended only as a supplement. The information is listed in as brief a form as possible for quick and easy reference. This way you will have more time to enjoy your stay, which is what we have tried to help you do.

1. At the border

Passport and visa requirements

A passport and Hungarian visa are required on entering Hungary. (The visa requirement is waived for citizens of Socialist countries, Austria, Finland, Malta, Nicaragua and Sweden, as well as for children under 14 accompanied by their parents.) A form must be filled out for the visa and you will need two 4×4 cm ($1\frac{1}{2} \times 1\frac{1}{2}$ in.) photos. The original form is left at the border on entering, and the carbon copy is handed over when leaving the country. The address of the place where you stayed must be registered on the carbon copy. Visas can be obtained in advance at any Hungarian diplomatic office, at the Budapest airport, at the international boat station or at the border when you arrive by car or bus. (Visas are not issued on trains.) Sight-seeing visas are issued at the airport to transit passengers.

If you lose your passport or have any other problems, you can turn to the appropriate department of the Hungarian police (KEA) at 12 Népköztársaság útja. Office hours are: Mon, Tues, Wed and Fri 9–12, Thurs 2–6.

Customs regulations

You can take the following into Hungary:

Duty free: 2 litres of wine, 1 litre of spirits, 250 cigarettes, 50 cigars, 250 gr. of tobacco and presents with a total value of under 6,000 forints.

Presents valued at up to 25,000 forints can be taken into the country without special permission but are subject to duty.

Special permission must be obtained to take in presents valued at over 25,000 forints. Valid veterinary certificates are required to take animals into the country, and weapons and firearms can be taken into the country only with proper permission from a Hungarian consulate.

Literature and video tapes containing excessive violence or pornography and certain political propaganda are not allowed into the country.

The following can be taken out of Hungary:

Duty free: 2 litres of wine, 1 litre of spirits, 250 cigarettes, 50 cigars, 250 gr. of tobacco and presents with a total value of under 3,000 forints.

Special permission must be obtained for works of art. For detailed information, call 160-170, extension 480.

Objects made of gold, silver or platinum, antiques, stamps, medicines and imported food and beverages are not allowed out of the country.

For more information on customs regulations call 326-943, or inquire in person at 11/B Szent István tér. Open: Mon–Thurs 8–5, Fri 8–4.

Currency

Only one hundred forints can be taken into and out of Hungary. There are no restrictions on foreign currency. There is an official exchange rate for the forint which does not vary within the country. There is no compulsory amount to be exchanged. Money can only be exchanged at officially designated places. In addition to cash, banks, large restaurants, hotels and shops will accept traveller's checks (from Austrian, US, French, Iraqi, Japanese, Italian and Swiss banks) and Eurocheque and credit cards (American Express, Bank of America, Carte Blanche, Diner's Club, Eurocard, and Universal Air Travel Plan). Forints can only be exchanged back into foreign currency at the airport and at the border when leaving the country. There is an upper limit of 50% of the amount exchanged, not to exceed 100 US dollars.

Traveling to Hungary

Planes from all over the world land at the Budapest airports, Ferihegy I and Ferihegy II. (International airlines arrive at Ferihegy I; the flights of Malév, the Hungarian airlines, arrive at Ferihegy II.) For information call: 572-122. To reserve seats call: 184-333 or inquire in person at the Malév counter in the lobbies of large hotels. Airport shuttle buses leave from the airport and from the Inner City (Engels tér) every half hour. (Time: 30–40 minutes.)

Trains connect Budapest with almost every major city in Europe. For information call: 228-049 or 228-056 or inquire in person at the passenger service office (MÁV Utasszolgálat, 35 Népköztársaság útja).

International bus connections can be made at Engels tér in the Inner City. For information call: 172-562.

There is also a hydrofoil which runs between Budapest and Vienna. In Budapest inquire at: International Boat Station (Nemzetközi hajóállomás), Belgrád rakpart. Tel.: 181-953 or 181-704. In Vienna inquire at: Praterkai, 11 Mexicoplatz 8. Tel.: 26-56-36 extensions 450, 451 and 452.

If the car you are driving runs on diesel, you must buy diesel coupons at the border which are not refundable on leaving. 86, 92 and 98 octane gasoline is available for cash throughout the country. Lead-free is also available at certain stations.

If your car breaks down: call the Hungarian Auto Club (Magyar Autóklub Mentőszolgálat) at 691-831 or 693-714 or inquire in person at 38/B Francia út in the 16th district. For information about road conditions call: Útinform: 227-052, 227-643, 222-238 or 229-831.

2. Practical Information for your stay

Accommodations

Hungarian hotels are rated using the internationally accepted categories. Several international hotel chains also have hotels in Hungary. Here is a brief list of recommended hotels.

Atrium Hyatt: 1051 Budapest, Roosevelt tér 2.
Tel.: 383-000 tx: 22-5484 *****

Duna Intercontinental: 1052 Budapest, Apáczai Csere János u. 4.
Tel.: 175-122 tx: 22-5277 *****

Hilton: 1014 Budapest, Hess András tér 1−3.
Tel.: 751-000 tx: 22-5984 *****

Thermal: 1138 Budapest, Margitsziget
Tel.: 321-100 tx: 22-5463 *****

Béke: 1067 Budapest, Lenin krt. 97.
Tel.: 323-300 tx: 22-5748 ****

Buda Penta: 1013 Budapest, Krisztina krt. 41−43.
Tel.: 566-333 tx: 22-5494 ****

Fórum: 1052 Budapest, Apáczai Csere János u. 12−14.
Tel.: 178-088 tx: 22-4178 ****

Gellért: 1111 Budapest, Szent Gellért tér 1.
Tel.: 852-200 tx: 22-4363 ****

Astoria: 1053 Budapest, Kossuth Lajos u. 19.
Tel.: 173-411 tx: 22-4205 ***

Grand Hotel Hungária: 1074 Budapest, Rákóczi út 90.
Tel.: 229-050 tx: 22-4987 ***

Palace: 1088 Budapest, Rákóczi út 43.
Tel.: 136-000 tx: 22-4217 ***

Taverna: 1052 Budapest, Váci u. 20.
Tel.: 384-999 tx: 22-7707 ***

Nemzeti: 1088 Budapest, József krt. 4.
Tel.: 339-160 **

Park: 1087 Budapest, Baross tér 10.
Tel.: 131-420 tx: 22-6247 **

Vörös Csillag: 1121 Budapest, Rege u. 21.
Tel.: 750-522 tx: 22-5125 **

Private rooms can also be rented in Hungarian homes (fizetővendég-szoba). The price, which includes the use of a bathroom, is much cheaper than that of a hotel room.

Youth Hostels are open during the summer months. For information contact: Express (Budapest V., Semmelweiss utca 4.) Tel.: 178-100.

Camp-sites are also located near the city and are rated according to international standards.

For more information on accommodations contact any Hungarian travel agency or Malév office. In Budapest contact the IBUSZ travel agency's 24-hour hotel service: 1052 Budapest, Petőfi Sándor tér 3. Tel.: 184-842.

Currency

See information under previous heading.

Information

Tourinform provides information for tourists in English, German, French and Italian. Tel.: 179-800.

Several western newspapers and magazines are available. The following are published in Hungary: Daily News —Neueste Nachrichten (published daily in English and German), Budapester Rundschau (published weekly in German), Programmes in Hungary (published monthly in English and German).

Radio: News in English, German and Russian after the 12 o'clock news in Hungarian on the Petőfi station. Danubius Radio broadcasts all day in German from April 1—September 29.

Post Office

Open Mon—Fri 8—6, Sat 8—2, closed Sundays. The post offices at the Eastern and Western Railway Stations (Keleti, Nyugati pályaudvar) are open round the clock.

Telephone: local calls from 7 a.m. to 6 p.m.: 2 forints for 3 minutes. From 6 p.m. to 7 a.m.: 2 forints for 6 minutes. Calls from hotels are more expensive.
Long-distance calls: within Hungary dial 06 then, after the tone, dial the area code and the number. To call outside Hungary dial 00 then, after the tone, dial the number of the country, the city code and finally the telephone number. To

call Hungary from other European countries: dial 36 for Hungary, then 1 for Budapest, then the number.
For more information on international long-distance calls: 186-977.

Time

Hungary belongs to the GMT+1 time zone. During summer time, which begins the end of March and lasts till the end of September, the clocks are turned ahead one hour.

Official holidays: January 1, April 4, Easter Monday, May 1, August 20, November 7 and December 25 and 26.

Getting Around in Budapest

For foreigners the simpliest way is to take a taxi. Tel.: Főtaxi: 222-222, Volántaxi: 666-666, Budataxi: 294-000, Citytaxi: 228-855.

Rent-a-car: Főtaxi–Hertz: 221-471, Volán–Europcar, Budget: 334-783, or at the desk at any hotel and Ferihegy Airport.

Public Transport: Budapest has an extremely well-organized public transport system. Maps are available at large ticket offices and at the last station on each line. You must buy a ticket in advance and punch it to validate it when you get on. The tickets are only valid in one direction and a new ticket must be used when transfering. Service is in general from 5 a.m. to 11 p.m. For more information call Fővinform: 171-173.

In Case of Emergency

First aid is free of charge in Hungary. Only the tests and treatments must be paid for. Doctor's offices are located in each district.

Emergency dental service: Dental Clinic (Fogászati Klinika) Budapest VIII., Mária u. 52. Tel.: 330-189.
Ambulance: Tel.: 04
Police: Tel.: 07
U.S. Embassy: Budapest V., Szabadság tér 12. Tel.: 124-224, 126-450.
British Embassy: Budapest V., Harmincad u. 6. Tel.: 182-888.

3. Eating out, cultural programs and events, shopping

Restaurants

Budapest has an extremely wide variety of restaurants. They generally serve lunch from 12 to 3 and dinner from 6 to 10, 12 or in some places even 4 a.m. Here are just a couple of suggested places:

Deluxe restaurants: Alabárdos, Gundel, 100 éves and the restaurants in the deluxe hotels.
Hungarian restaurants: Ménes Csárda, Margitkert, Mátyás Pince.
Small restaurants serving delicious food in cosy surroundings in the medium range: Kis-Buda, Híd, Sípos Halászkert (fish), Arany Szarvas (game).

Cafés and pastry shops

Old-style: Gerbeaud, Ruszwurm, Lukács.
Modern: The Viennese Café at the Fórum Hotel, the Zsolnay Café at the Béke Hotel.
Open at night: Pierrot Piano Bar, Galéria Drink Bar.

Beer Halls

Fregatt, Kaltenberg, Radeberger Sörpatika.

Nightlife

Nightclubs with a floor show: Moulin Rouge, Maxim, Lido, Budapest Orfeum.
Discotheques with a floor show: Havanna, Horoszkóp Bár.
Discotheques with no floor show: Novotel, Mediterrán Disco (Thursdays), Halászbástya and Fortuna Bár.

Cultural Programs

Museums: usually open from 10−6. (Special hours have been noted in the book.)
Music events: Budapest has two opera houses and three concert halls. The simpliest way to get tickets is through your hotel or at the central ticket office: Színházak Központi Jegyirodája, Budapest VI., 18 Népköztársaság útja. Tel.: 120-000.

Annual Events

Spring Festival: generally held in late March. Features Hungarian and international guests from the world of music, the fine arts, the theater and folklore.
BNV (Budapest International Fair): an international exhibition, usually held in mid-May.
1 May: Procession, May Day fair, arts and crafts fairs, concerts and performances all day in the City Park and the Tabán Park.
July−August: A varied selection of open-air theater performances and concerts.
20 August, Constitution Day: A water and air parade during the day and a fireworks display in the evening.
Late August: Formula I Race at Mogyoród near Budapest.
Late September: International fair featuring consumer goods.

25 September–31 October: Budapest Art Weeks: A wide range of cultural programs.

Shopping

Stores in Hungary are usually open Mon–Fri 10–6, Thurs 10–8 and Sat 9–1. Stores will generally take only Hungarian currency, but large stores, essencially those catering to tourists, do accept credit cards. You can find Intertourist Shops in the hotels, which accept payment in foreign currency only. The goods purchased in these shops can be taken out of the country duty-free when you show your receipt. Folk art shops and antique shops are located throughout the Castle District and the Inner City. Prices are generally the same, but quality varies. Some are open on Saturdays and Sundays.

What to Buy in Hungary? Folk art, books and records, which are much cheaper than in Western Europe; Herend porcelain, one of the most famous and most valuable porcelains in the world; and Helia-D cosmetics.

Note:

Note:

Note:

Responsible publisher: Director of the Téka Publisher, Drucker Tibor
Printed by: Ságvári Nyomda (88.0316)
General manager: György Mogyorósi